DESTINED
for
GREATNESS

McDougal & Associates

Servants of Christ and Stewards of the
Mysteries of God

DESTINED

for

GREATNESS

by

Dr. Abiola Idowu

Published by:

McDougal & Associates
www,ThePublishedWord.com

McDougal & Associates is dedicated to spreading the Gospel of the Lord Jesus Christ to as many people as possible in the shortest time possible.

ISBN: 978-1-964665-20-7

Printed on demand in the U.S., the U.K., Australia, and the UAE
For Worldwide Distribution

DEDICATION

This book is dedicated to all Kingdom citizens destined by God for greatness through the blood of Jesus Christ.

CONTENTS

And the LORD shall make thee the head, and not the tail; and thou shalt be above only, and thou shalt not be beneath; if that thou hearken unto the commandments of the LORD thy God, which I command thee this day, to observe and to do them.

— Deuteronomy 28:13

INTRODUCTION
(WHAT WE NEED TO UNDERSTAND)

It is obvious that God wants you to rise and accomplish the dream He put in your heart, "obvious," I say, because His Word clearly establishes that fact:

> *For I know the thoughts that I think toward you, saith the LORD, thoughts of peace, and not of evil, to give you an expected end.*   Jeremiah 29:11

The pressures of life have nothing to do with the program of God. For you, all pressures are temporal; only the Word of God is eternal. He called to you in Isaiah 60:1-3:

> *Arise, shine; for thy light is come, and the glory of the LORD is risen upon thee.*

For, behold, the darkness shall cover the earth, and gross darkness the people: but the LORD shall arise upon thee, and his glory shall be seen upon thee. And the Gentiles shall come to thy light, and kings to the brightness of thy rising.

Any pressure you feel is proof that pleasure is coming, and because you are a glory carrier in Christ, this, for you, is a season of good news. Again, God promised:

And the LORD shall make thee the head, and not the tail; and thou shalt be above only, and thou shalt not be beneath; if that thou hearken unto the commandments of the LORD thy God, which I command thee this day, to observe and to do them.   Deuteronomy 28:13

This day the Scriptures can be fulfilled in your life if you will only believe and receive. Receive what? Receive what God has promised. He hates stagnation, and because of it, He told the children of Israel:

You have stayed long enough on this mountain. Turn and resume your journey. Deuteronomy 1:6-7, AMP

Their Promised Land was waiting, and they needed to stop wasting the resources that already had their name on them. However, when, in time, the land was subdued through Joshua, for some, it seemed their situation had not changed at all:

Then the whole congregation of the Israelites assembled at Shiloh [in the tribal territory of Ephraim], and set up the Tent of Meeting there; and the land was subdued before them. There remained among the Israelites seven tribes who had not yet divided their inheritance. So Joshua asked them, "How long will you put off entering to take possession of the land which the Lord, *the God of your fathers, has given you?"* Joshua 18:1-3, AMP

In the same way, today, even though Jesus

11

long ago paid the price for our greatness
and all things belong to Him and those who
believe on Him, the situation of many "believers" has not changed. How long before
you receive your healing, your promotion,
your baby, your prosperity, your new anointing? You are destined for greatness, and the
land has already been subdued. Enter in and
possess what is yours by inheritance.

Jesus has already paid the price:

> *Then one of the [twenty-four] elders
> said to me, "Stop weeping! Look closely,
> the Lion of the tribe of Judah, the Root
> of David, has overcome and conquered!
> He can open the scroll and [break] its
> seven seals."*   Revelation 5:5, AMP

He *"has overcome and conquered."* Yes, He
said:

> *All things that the Father hath are mine:
> therefore said I, that he shall take of
> mine, and shall shew it unto you.*
> >   John 16:15

This is confirmed in Romans 8:17:

And if children, then heirs; heirs of God,
and joint-heirs with Christ.

So, what are you still waiting for? It's time to move to your next level in Jesus' name. Many are slack, not because they don't want the next level and the manifestation of their glory, but because they don't know the truth, and the enemy has lied to them about their inheritance.

So, how do we move from here to there? That is the purpose and message of this book. You are *Destined for Greatness,* but there are things you must understand and put into practice in order to become outstanding. Let's get started.

Dr. Abiola Idowu
Jacksonville, Florida

CHAPTER 1

THINGS YOU MUST UNDERSTAND TO ACHIEVE GREATNESS

Here are some things you must understand as a believer in Christ if you really want God's best for your life:

UNDERSTAND YOUR ORIGIN

Jacob called for his sons and said, "Gather around, and I will tell you what will happen to you in the future:

"Judah, your brothers will praise you.
You hold your enemies by the neck.
Your brothers will bow down before you.

Judah is like a lion,
Killing his victim and returning to his den,
Stretching out and lying down.
No one dares disturb him.
Judah will hold the royal scepter,
And his descendants will always rule.
Nations will bring him tribute
And bow in obedience before him.
He ties his young donkey to a grapevine,
To the very best of the vines.
He washes his clothes in blood-red wine."

Genesis 49:1 and 8-12, GNT

You were created by divine design and destined for the top. But perhaps, although the family you belonged to had a track record of greatness, you felt you were too insignificant to break that record. Understand this: every person born into a royal family is either a prince or a princess, regardless of what he or she feels. Achieving greatness has nothing to do with feelings. We're talking about facts. Understand this about yourself.

After the patriarchs received the blessing and prospered in it, even when it seemed difficult or impossible, it came Jacob's turn to release the blessing before he passed on. This was the same blessing God had given to Adam in the beginning. In this passage, we can see him blessing his children, particularly Judah.

From this scripture, we can catch a glimpse of the future God had prepared for Judah, a future blessed with honor, victory, dignity, royalty, leadership, prosperity, and wealth.

God had spoken a similar thing through Moses:

> *And this is the blessing, wherewith Moses the man of God blessed the children of Israel before his death.*
> *And this is the blessing of Judah: and he said, Hear, LORD, the voice of Judah, and bring him unto his people: let his hands be sufficient for him; and be thou an help to him from his enemies.*
> Deuteronomy 33:1 and 7

This was a prophecy that Jesus came to fulfill, and the Bible called Him the Lion of the

Tribe of Judah (see Revelation 5:5). Through covenant, everyone who is saved through Christ belongs to Judah's tribe. Romans 8:29 calls Him *"the firstborn among many brethren,"* and Colossians 1:17-19 confirms Him as *"the firstborn."* What does that mean? It means that He was not the last or the only one destined for this blessing. You can have it too. By redemption you are connected to this same tribe of Judah. You have an inheritance, so don't lose your identity. Every member of this tribe is destined to rise, and it's your turn.

This prophecy came to pass in the life of Jesus, even when He was taken into Hell. Even there, the neck of the devil was delivered to Him. He said:

> *I am he that liveth, and was dead; and, behold, I am alive for evermore, Amen; and have the keys of hell and of death.*
>   Revelation 1:18

Amen! You have been born by faith into a glorious family, and your rise to greatness is at hand. See this in Judges 1:1-3:

18

Now after the death of Joshua it came to pass, that the children of Israel asked the LORD, saying, Who shall go up for us against the Canaanites first, to fight against them?

And the LORD said, Judah shall go up: behold, I have delivered the land into his hand.

And Judah said unto Simeon his brother, Come up with me into my lot, that we may fight against the Canaanites; and I likewise will go with thee into thy lot. So Simeon went with him.

The name *Joshua* has the same meaning as the name Jesus—savior, deliverer. Therefore, after the death of Jesus, it's your turn to take over. You must now move to the next level, you must claim your inheritance, and your glory must be revealed in and through the name of Jesus Christ.

UNDERSTAND THE NEED TO KEEP HOPE ALIVE

To be hopeless is to be lifeless. When hope

is dead, faith has nothing to work with. No matter what is happening, keep your hope alive. God is not a man that He should lie. He declared:

> *Behold, I am the LORD, the God of all flesh: is there any thing too hard for me?* Jeremiah 32:27

Don't lose hope. When hope is dead, you lose your rightful place. The Bible says there is always hope:

> *For there is hope of a tree, if it be cut down, that it will sprout again, and that the tender branch thereof will not cease. Though the root thereof wax old in the earth, and the stock thereof die in the ground; yet through the scent of water it will bud, and bring forth boughs like a plant.* Job 14:7-9

"Through the scent of water," that tree comes back. And you are coming back. It's not over yet. When you entertain the comfort of the

sacred Scriptures, hope comes rushing back, and faith has something to work with:

> *For whatsoever things were written aforetime were written for our learning, that we through patience and comfort of the scriptures might have hope.*
> Romans 15:4

Abraham believed, hoping against hope, and the miracle happened. If you are hopeless, you limit the way God can intervene in your case. When you are hopeless, you can't fight, you can't pray, and you become depressed:

> *And he said unto her, Daughter, be of good comfort: thy faith hath made thee whole; go in peace.*
> *While he yet spake, there cometh one from the ruler of the synagogue's house, saying to him, Thy daughter is dead; trouble not the Master.*
> *But when Jesus heard it, he answered him, saying, Fear not: believe only, and she shall be made whole.*

> *And when he came into the house, he suffered no man to go in, save Peter, and James, and John, and the father and the mother of the maiden. And all wept, and bewailed her: but he said, Weep not; she is not dead, but sleepeth. And they laughed him to scorn, knowing that she was dead. And he put them all out, and took her by the hand, and called, saying, Maid, arise. And her spirit came again, and she arose straightway: and he commanded to give her meat. And her parents were astonished: but he charged them that they should tell no man what was done.* Luke 8:48-56

The people around you will want to talk you out of your miracle, your greatness, just as these "sympathizers" laughed at Jesus. But the hope He extended brought forth faith, and when faith is present, God begins to work His miracles.

Hopelessness is like saying, "God is dead," and I tell you: God is alive, and He wants to turn your situation into an opportunity to exalt His name. Don't give up on yourself and don't give up on God.

If what you have been asking God to do has not yet come, don't allow your hope to die:

> *I will stand upon my watch, and set me upon the tower, and will watch to see what he will say unto me, and what I shall answer when I am reproved. And the LORD answered me, and said, Write the vision, and make it plain upon tables, that he may run that readeth it. For the vision is yet for an appointed time, but at the end it shall speak, and not lie: though it tarry, wait for it; because it will surely come, it will not tarry.*
>
> Habakkuk 2:1-3

"It shall speak," and though it tarry, it will surely come to pass. Therefore, rejoice for your dream is coming true. Now is your time.

UNDERSTAND THAT YOU ARE UNDER A TOTALLY NEW SYSTEM OF GOVERNMENT

We have been told that we are suffering for the sin of Adam and Eve, but that is not the whole truth. After Adam sinned, Noah was blessed, and it was the same as at the beginning:

> *And God blessed Noah and his sons, and said unto them, Be fruitful, and multiply, and replenish the earth. And the fear of you and the dread of you shall be upon every beast of the earth, and upon every fowl of the air, upon all that moveth upon the earth, and upon all the fishes of the sea; into your hand are they delivered. Every moving thing that liveth shall be meat for you; even as the green herb have I given you all things.* Genesis 9:1-3

Then why are we suffering? We are suffering because of ignorance, because of disobedience to God's Word, because of the system we have set up for ourselves—or maybe because of all three.

After the flood, God backtracked and reset things in order as they had been in the beginning, but then the sons of Noah—Ham and Japheth—teamed up to declare independence from God's sovereign reign upon the earth. They set up a kingdom with rules of its own and declared their independence from God, and confusion quickly set in:

And the whole earth was of one language, and of one speech. And it came to pass, as they journeyed from the east, that they found a plain in the land of Shinar; and they dwelt there. And they said one to another, Go to, let us make brick, and burn them thoroughly. And they had brick for stone, and slime had they for morter. And they said, Go to, let us build us a city and a tower, whose top may reach unto heaven; and let us make us a name, lest we be scattered abroad upon the face of the whole earth.

And the LORD came down to see the city and the tower, which the children of men builded. And the LORD said, Behold, the people is one, and they have all one language; and this they begin to do: and now nothing will be restrained

25

> *from them, which they have imagined*
> *to do.*   Genesis 11:1-6

Any government official who thinks they can fix things without God's help is Babylon, and all their efforts will eventually lead to utter confusion. Unfortunately, the Church, which was intended to set the pace for the rest of the world, has itself joined Babylon. Be it Communism, socialism, monarchy, or even democracy, when God is not at the center, it will eventually crash.

God called Abraham out of the world's system and prospered him and sustained him, even in time of famine. What happens on this Earth never affects the government of God. He rules over all things. Every time men rebelled against His system (because they wanted to make a name for themselves), God took care of His people, Israel, and everything they needed was supplied to them supernaturally, including their health. Then, sadly, they, too, became rebellious and decided, "We need a king over us like other nations." The saddest thing is they didn't bother to check on how those nations that had declared independence from God were doing and, therefore, suffered the same fate.

God spoke to the prophet Samuel:

> *And the LORD said unto Samuel, Hearken unto the voice of the people in all that they say unto thee: for they have not rejected thee, but they have rejected me, that I should not reign over them.*
>
> 1 Samuel 8:7

The Kingdom those people were rejecting is the same Kingdom Jesus came to proclaim:

> *From that time Jesus began to preach, and to say, Repent: for the kingdom of heaven is at hand.*   Matthew 4:17

The religious leaders of Jesus' day were the first to oppose Him. How foolish, for God's Kingdom promotes and lifts up its common citizens, just as it does their King:

Here it is again:

> *And the* LORD *shall make thee the head, and not the tail; and thou shalt be above only, and thou shalt not be beneath; if that thou hearken unto the commandments of the* LORD *thy God, which I command thee this day, to observe and to do them.*   Deuteronomy 28:13

Jesus said:

> *Ye are the salt of the earth: but if the salt have lost his savour, wherewith shall it be salted? it is thenceforth good for nothing, but to be cast out, and to be trodden under foot of men. Ye are the light of the world. A city that is set on an hill cannot be hid.*   Matthew 5:13-14

Even as men ignored or opposed Jesus, He kept declaring that what He was preaching to them was the will of their heavenly Father, God. He capped this by teaching, *"Seek ye first":*

(For after all these things do the Gentiles seek:) for your heavenly Father knoweth that ye have need of all these things. But seek ye first the kingdom of God, and his righteousness; and all these things shall be added unto you. Matthew 6:32-33

As a result, when your job takes the place of God, you are building Babylon. When your money or your possessions take the place of God, it will all end in confusion.

God's Kingdom is based upon His Word and is independent of the world system. If you need a healthy life, then go to the Department of Health in God's Kingdom and see what it has to offer. He said:

And ye shall serve the Lord your God, and he shall bless thy bread, and thy water; and I will take sickness away from the midst of thee. Exodus 23:25

If you believe it, than claim it. Say, "By His stripes, I am healed" (see 1 Peter 2:24), and seal it with the authority of the name of Jesus Christ.

If you need wealth, the Kingdom Department of Finances handles that:

> *Will a man rob God? Yet ye have robbed me. But ye say, Wherein have we robbed thee? In tithes and offerings. Ye are cursed with a curse: for ye have robbed me, even this whole nation. Bring ye all the tithes into the storehouse, that there may be meat in mine house, and prove me now herewith, saith the LORD of hosts, if I will not open you the windows of heaven, and pour you out a blessing, that there shall not be room enough to receive it.*   Malachi 3:8-10

Your tithes and your seed offerings (not your job) are the key to your prosperity.

If you desire long life, then do what God says. Honor your father and your mother (both physical and spiritual fathers), keep your tongue from speaking guile (see Psalm 34:13), and stand in faith, and the promise will be yours. That is the very best insurance.

If you want all-round victory in life, then go to God's Department of Defense:

> *Out of the mouth of babes and sucklings hast thou ordained strength because of thine enemies, that thou mightest still the enemy and the avenger.* Psalm 8:2

Yes, your praises immobilize the enemy.

If you want to carry the power of God, then live a life of purity:

> *Follow peace with all men, and holiness, without which no man shall see the Lord.* Hebrews 12:14

Everything you need is in the Word. Learn it and follow it, and your life will reflect it.

Are you still interested in manifesting the glory of God upon your life and achieving your God-ordained destiny? Then let's get to work doing the will of God in the name of Jesus Christ.

You are *Destined for Greatness,* but there are things you must understand and put into practice in order to become outstanding.

CHAPTER 2

SECRETS TO LIVING AN OUTSTANDING LIFE

But God, who is rich in mercy, for his great love wherewith he loved us, even when we were dead in sins, hath quickened us together with Christ, (by grace ye are saved;) and hath raised us up together, and made us sit together in heavenly places in Christ Jesus: that in the ages to come he might shew the exceeding riches of his grace in his kindness toward us through Christ Jesus.

Ephesians 2:4-7

You and I are ordained to produce results that amaze the world around us because of who we are, where we are seated, and who is standing by us. We are God's workmanship created in Christ Jesus. We are His Bride. We are His weapons of war. The Bible says:

> *If God be for us, who can be against us?* Romans 8:31

Who indeed? Never ever forget that. Our superiority is based upon our position in Christ. There was nothing spectacular about acacia wood until it was fashioned into the Ark of the Covenant. Although the wood was covered inside and out with gold, it was Who lived there that changed the story. To Him, every force of darkness and every challenge of life had to bow, and now He lives in you. That makes you the boss.

> *But now, after that ye have known God, or rather are known of God, how turn ye again to the weak and beggarly elements, whereunto ye desire again to be in bondage?* Galatians 4:9

"The weak and beggarly elements" of this world, including its culture and traditions, offer us

only *"bondage."* Having experienced the liber-
ating force of God's Kingdom, how could we
ever turn back to these *"beggarly elements":*

> *Don't let anyone capture you with
> empty philosophies and high-sounding
> nonsense that come from human think-
> ing and from the spiritual powers of
> this world, rather than from Christ. For
> in Christ lives all the fullness of God in
> a human body. So you also are complete
> through your union with Christ, who
> is the head over every ruler and author-
> ity.* Colossians 2:8-10, NLT

The world is waiting for our manifestation, and we cannot afford to disappoint.
God's power and glory in us is the manifestation or demonstration of Heaven on Earth
that will cause men and women to envy our
position.

Jesus taught us to pray:

> *After this manner therefore pray ye: Our
> Father which art in heaven, Hallowed be*

> *thy name. Thy kingdom come, Thy will*
> *be done in earth, as it is in heaven.*
> Matthew 6:9-10

God's original plan, before the foundation of the world, was that His Son, Jesus Christ, would come to Earth to bring this dream to reality. That's why we are not just Christians; we are little Christs because we live in Him, and we have our being in Him:

> *For in him we live, and move, and have*
> *our being; as certain also of your own*
> *poets have said, For we are also his off-*
> *spring. Forasmuch then as we are the*
> *offspring of God, we ought not to think*
> *that the Godhead is like unto gold, or*
> *silver, or stone, graven by art and man's*
> *device.* Acts 17:28-29

John went as far as proclaiming, *"As he is, so are we in this world"* (1 John 4:17). Theoretically, we may be holy and untouchable by any evil, but that must be acknowledged if we are to see it manifested:

*That the communication of thy faith
may become effectual by the acknowledging of every good thing which is in
you in Christ Jesus.*   Philemon 1:6

YOU HAVE UNLIMITED
POTENTIAL INSIDE OF YOU

*But we have this treasure in earthen
vessels, that the excellency of the power
may be of God, and not of us.*
                    2 Corinthians 4:7

Not one of us is empty. It's just that many
have not yet acknowledged the treasure
they carry. Thank God for what we have
seen, but there is much more packaged inside of us, just waiting to come forth.

When Gideon was discouraged and paralyzed by fear, God said to him:

*The LORD is with thee, thou mighty man
of valour.
Go in this thy might, and thou shalt save
Israel from the hand of the Midianites.*
                    Judges 6:12 and 14

That must have sounded absurd based on Gideon's situation. But we have to go far beyond IQ, gifts, and talents, for we have the Holy Ghost, the Custodian of all knowledge. *"The Spirit searcheth all things, yea, the deep things of God"*:

> *But as it is written, Eye hath not seen, nor ear heard, neither have entered into the heart of man, the things which God hath prepared for them that love him. But God hath revealed them unto us by his Spirit: for the Spirit searcheth all things, yea, the deep things of God.*
> 1 Corinthians 2:9-10

Stop lying about God. He gave you the Holy Ghost, and He is inside us right now. No wonder Paul could say:

> *I can do all things through Christ which strengtheneth me.*   Philippians 4:13

You, too, can *"do all things through Christ."*

THE POWER IN THE NAME OF JESUS IS YOUR TOOL OF OPERATION

The word *baptism* had been minimized and misunderstood in our day. To be baptized means "to immerse, soak or bury a thing." You have been baptized into the name of Jesus Christ, and it is no longer what we think we should have. His life is now our life.

The all-powerful name of Jesus rules the world. Use it to push the devil out of your territory:

> *And being found in fashion as a man, he humbled himself, and became obedient unto death, even the death of the cross. Wherefore God also hath highly exalted him, and given him a name which is above every name: that at the name of Jesus every knee should bow, of things in heaven, and things in earth, and things under the earth.*
>
> Philippians 2:8-10

And these signs shall follow them that believe; In my name shall they cast out devils; they shall speak with new tongues. Mark 16:17

This is not prayer; it is authority. It is using Jesus' name as a police officer uses his or her authority to arrest a criminal or to enforce the law. You have authority over every unseen force of darkness and can destroy their hold in the name of Jesus Christ. He said:

Behold, I give unto you power to tread on serpents and scorpions, and over all the power of the enemy: and nothing shall by any means hurt you.

Luke 10:19

John wrote to the early churches:

Ye are of God, little children, and have overcome them: because greater is he that is in you, than he that is in the world. 1 John 4:4

The enemy is not nearly as strong as he thinks he is. He uses fear and lies to deceive. He purports to use physical evidence to substantiate his claims, but God says you will *not* die of sickness and disease:

> *And the LORD will take away from thee all sickness, and will put none of the evil diseases of Egypt, which thou knowest, upon thee; but will lay them upon all them that hate thee.*
>
> Deuteronomy 7:15

STEP OUT OF YOUR FLESH AND LIVE BY THE WORD

> *For they that are after the flesh do mind the things of the flesh; but they that are after the Spirit the things of the Spirit. For to be carnally minded is death; but to be spiritually minded is life and peace. Because the carnal mind is enmity against God: for it is not subject to the law of God, neither indeed can be. So then they that are in the flesh cannot*

> *please God. But ye are not in the flesh,*
> *but in the Spirit, if so be that the Spirit*
> *of God dwell in you. Now if any man*
> *have not the Spirit of Christ, he is none*
> *of his.* Romans 8:5-9

As humans, we are so conscious of our flesh and feelings, all too often more than we are conscious of what God's Word says. No matter what you see or feel, it is temporal, and you can't depend on it:

> *For the flesh lusteth against the Spirit,*
> *and the Spirit against the flesh: and*
> *these are contrary the one to the other:*
> *so that ye cannot do the things that ye*
> *would.* Galatians 5:17

Stand your ground by faith, and you will overcome the flesh through prayer and meditation. Ultimately, the Word of God is far more powerful than the flesh:

> *Heaven and earth shall pass away, but*
> *my words shall not pass away.*
> Matthew 24:35

So shall my word be that goeth forth out of my mouth: it shall not return unto me void, but it shall accomplish that which I please, and it shall prosper in the thing whereto I sent it.　　　Isaiah 55:11

Know the Word and stand on the Word, and you will be well on your way to fulfilling your God-given destiny.

YOU ARE THE KING'S REPRESENTATIVE HERE ON EARTH AND MUST RATIFY EACH OF YOUR DEMANDS AND DREAMS WITH YOUR SIGNATURE

The potency of every document is a signature. With a signature appended, you have a legal document that can stand any test. God has spoken, but you must sign to make what He has said yours:

My heart is inditing a good matter: I speak of the things which I have made touching the king: my tongue is the pen of a ready writer.　　　Psalm 45:1

43

For verily I say unto you, That whosoever shall say unto this mountain, Be thou removed, and be thou cast into the sea; and shall not doubt in his heart, but shall believe that those things which he saith shall come to pass; he shall have whatsoever he saith.   Mark 11:23

God is all-powerful, but He insists upon your cooperation in the process. Many speak all the wrong things, not agreeing with God at all. He said, "You have wearied Me with your words":

Ye have wearied the LORD with your words. Yet ye say, Wherein have we wearied him? When ye say, Every one that doeth evil is good in the sight of the LORD, and he delighteth in them; or, Where is the God of judgment?   Malachi 2:17

Wake up and sign the document. It has been settled in Heaven, but you must settle it on Earth in and through the name of Jesus Christ. Ratify your healing by speaking it. Do the same for your longevity, your strength, your abundance, your marriage, or the peace of your children. It does not matter how things look. Sign the document by speaking your desire into reality in the name of Jesus Christ.

LIVE BY DESIGN AND NOT BY DEFAULT

Life was designed by God with you in mind:

> *There be many that say, Who will shew us any good? LORD, lift thou up the light of thy countenance upon us.*
> Psalm 4:6

All of Heaven's resources have been placed at your disposal for the fulfillment of God's dream for this Universe, and you are the principle actor. The mistake many make is to think that God created everything for Himself. No, He did it for you. You were created for His glory. The pipe that carries heavenly water to you never goes dry, and God doesn't need dollars, He never uses automobiles, and He never flies on airplanes. Trust Him:

> *Charge them that are rich in this world, that they be not highminded, nor trust in uncertain riches, but in the living God, who giveth us richly all things to enjoy*   1 Timothy 6:17

Having an understanding of how to tap into your portion of your Father's inheritance can bring fulfillment into your life:

> *Moreover the profit of the earth is for all: the king himself is served by the field.*
> Ecclesiastes 5:9

It is all made plain in God's blueprint. He said:

> *For I know the thoughts that I think toward you, saith the* LORD*, thoughts of peace, and not of evil, to give you an expected end.*   Jeremiah 29:11

You are not just incidental to the picture; the entire story is about you:

> *And the* LORD *God took the man, and put him into the garden of Eden to dress it and to keep it.* Genesis 2:15
> *For thus saith the* LORD *that created the heavens; God himself that formed the earth and made it; he hath established it, he created it not in vain, he formed it to be inhabited: I am the* LORD*; and there is none else.* Isaiah 45:18

God trusted you and me and said, *"Let them have dominion"* (Genesis 1:26). Jesus said of us:

> *Ye are the salt of the earth: but if the salt have lost his savour, wherewith shall it be salted? it is thenceforth good for nothing, but to be cast out, and to be trodden under foot of men. Ye are the light of the world. A city that is set on an hill cannot be hid.* Matthew 5:13-14

This establishes the fact that all things are in place for your sake. Jesus also told us in the Parable of the Minas:

> *And he called his ten servants, and delivered them ten pounds, and said unto them, Occupy till I come.*
>
> Luke 19:13

Each of these ten servants was told the same thing: *"Occupy till I come."* This means you already have loaded in you what you need to make the most of life. You have enough to occupy until Jesus returns. Now, make use of it.

God had a plan to get this planet back from the hands of the devil, and the plan was to use His people. He desires to reign through you:

> *And it shall come to pass in the last days, that the mountain of the LORD's house shall be established in the top of the mountains, and shall be exalted above the hills; and all nations shall*

flow unto it. And many people shall go and say, Come ye, and let us go up to the mountain of the Lord, to the house of the God of Jacob; and he will teach us of his ways, and we will walk in his paths: for out of Zion shall go forth the law, and the word of the Lord from Jerusalem. And he shall judge among the nations, and shall rebuke many people: and they shall beat their swords into plowshares, and their spears into pruninghooks: nation shall not lift up sword against nation, neither shall they learn war any more.   Isaiah 2:2-4

This world is destined to be ruled by the Lord Jesus through His faithful servants. If all this was to be done automatically without any input on your part, then there would be no need for faith or for wisdom. You need to know what to do to put your faith into action so that you can make the most of life and fulfill your God-given destiny.

UNDERSTAND YOUR PURPOSE

Purpose is the reason for a thing. It is the dream, the desire in the heart of the manufacturer. Without a purpose, there could be no production. When a man or woman has not discovered his or her purpose, he or she is born but not really living. Living starts when a purpose is discovered. You have been predestinated to be justified and glorified, for God has a great purpose for you:

> *For whom he did foreknow, he also did predestinate to be conformed to the image of his Son, that he might be the firstborn among many brethren. Moreover whom he did predestinate, them he also called: and whom he called, them he also justified: and whom he justified, them he also glorified.*
>
> Romans 8:29-30

If you are born again, you are a child of destiny. Billions of people now call this planet home, so God didn't need more people. He needed *you*, and you came here to do something specific and grand.

You may not have discovered your purpose yet, but I guarantee you that purpose was in the mind of the Creator, the Manufacturer, before He brought you forth. Therefore, you cannot come here and do what everybody else is doing. You were designed to fulfill an eternal plan.

You don't create your own purpose or dream it up. It was in the mind of your Maker, and it is clearly defined. Find that purpose, and you will thrive.

This is why God has placed His Spirit in you, and you must not be lost in the crowd. Your purpose is what gives meaning to your life. When you understand this, you will be safe, even in the midst of storms. Knowing your purpose will keep you stable. Plans may change, but purpose never does. This can keep you focused and simplify your life. It can also keep you motivated.

Fulfillment in life starts with the discovery of your purpose. The Bible clearly states that where there is no purpose, people perish:

Where there is no vision, the people per-
ish: but he that keepeth the law, happy
is he.   Proverbs 29:18

You are uniquely unique, and it's time to reveal your uniqueness to your world. Everything and everybody is created with a purpose, and that purpose will give your life meaning and keep you alive:

Now Joshua was old and stricken in
years; and the LORD said unto him,
Thou art old and stricken in years, and
there remaineth yet very much land to
be possessed.   Joshua 13:1

You are not permitted to die until your purpose is fulfilled. Never allow the enemy to cheat you out of God's plan.

UNDERSTAND YOUR POTENTIAL

Potentials are hidden abilities, what you are designed to become that you have not yet become. God put potential in you. When

He created you, before He released you into this Earth, He placed inside of you all that is needed to perform the five-fold blessing of your assignment:

> *And God blessed them, and God said unto them, Be fruitful, and multiply, and replenish the earth, and subdue it: and have dominion over the fish of the sea, and over the fowl of the air, and over every living thing that moveth upon the earth.*   Genesis 1:28

"Be fruitful," "multiply," "replenish the earth," "subdue it," and *"have dominion."* That's your calling, your purpose, your potential. The Bible says:

> *He is the Rock, his work is perfect: for all his ways are judgment: a God of truth and without iniquity, just and right is he.*   Deuteronomy 32:4

God is our Rock, His work is perfect, all His ways are just, and you are the work of His hands. Anything contrary to that is from the enemy and is a lie. This promise, this truth, is there, but until you place a demand on it, it cannot manifest. You must step out of the boat, take responsibility, and dare to do new things.

The only limit to your potential is your own ignorance, lack of faith, and failure to act on what you know. Jesus Christ said:

> *Verily, verily, I say unto you, He that believeth on me, the works that I do shall he do also; and greater works than these shall he do; because I go unto my Father.* John 14:12

The world is waiting for the greater works from you.

Adam was made in the image of God, and yet it was never automatic for Him to manifest dominion over creation. God had clearly placed a demand on Him, but it was up to Adam to fulfill it.

When God brought all the animals to Adam and told him to give them names, He didn't provide Adam with a list to choose from or even training on how to do it. He knew Adam had what he needed to do it. When you think life is treating you rough, this may be a test to see what's inside of you.

In Matthew 17, people brought *"a lunatick"* to the disciples and, with him, a demand they couldn't handle. Jesus was disappointed in them. Like you and me, they were called to function like Jesus did. It was not that they *could not* but that they *did not*. Jesus had already given them authority over all devils and to heal all diseases:

> *And when he had called unto him his twelve disciples, he gave them power against unclean spirits, to cast them out, and to heal all manner of sickness and all manner of disease.*
>
> Matthew 10:1

The world was amazed to see the operation of wisdom and power in His life, and they called Him *"the only begotten Son"* of God (John 1:14 and 18, etc.). After His resurrection, however, He was now *"the firstborn"* among many:

> *To the general assembly and church of the firstborn, which are written in heaven, and to God the Judge of all, and to the spirits of just men made perfect.*
> Hebrews 12:23

Don't be deceived by your covering which is often called "the body of Christ." Look to Him who is the Greater One inside of you:

> *Ye are of God, little children, and have overcome them: because greater is he that is in you, than he that is in the world.* 1 John 4:4

Ephesians 2:6 tells us that we are seated *"in heaven places."* Therefore, nothing from Hell or this Earth can be allowed to hinder you. Stand your ground. You are born of God, so you can overcome the world.

MAKE A DECISION TO BE OUTSTANDING

The most powerful tool in the hand of any believer is the ability to make a decision. Your decision will determine how far you can go in life. Your decision is the key that can activate your purpose and your potential. No one is ever rewarded for good intentions but, instead, for decisive actions. Your actions concerning your life's destiny will be a result of your decisions. The Bible says, *"Choose you this day whom you will serve"*:

> *And if it seem evil unto you to serve the Lord, choose you this day whom ye will serve; whether the gods which your fathers served that were on the other side of the flood, or the gods of the Amorites, in whose land ye dwell: but as for me and my house, we will serve the Lord.*
> Joshua 24:15

> *I call heaven and earth to record this day against you, that I have set before you life*

57

> *and death, blessing and cursing: therefore*
> *choose life, that both thou and thy seed*
> *may live.*   Deuteronomy 30:19

"I have set before you life and death." The wonderful thing about life is that we get to make decisions about its outcome. If you make a conscious decision not to live an average life, God will stand by you. Your decision to win is what God is waiting for.

Imagine, God was with the children of Israel, and yet for forty days Goliath taunted their armies, and they did nothing. This taunting ended only when David arrived and made a decision to activate the covenant they had with God. The Word declares:

> *The LORD shall open unto thee his*
> *good treasure, the heaven to give the*
> *rain unto thy land in his season, and*
> *to bless all the work of thine hand: and*
> *thou shalt lend unto many nations, and*
> *thou shalt not borrow. And the LORD*
> *shall make thee the head, and not the*
> *tail; and thou shalt be above only, and*

thou shalt not be beneath; if that thou hearken unto the commandments of the LORD thy God, which I command thee this day, to observe and to do them.
                    Deuteronomy 28:12-13

The promise is there, but you have to make a decision to activate it. God won't make these decisions for you:

A man's heart deviseth his way: but the LORD directeth his steps.
                              Proverbs 16:9

We should make plans, counting on God to direct us. What you make out of life is up to you, not God. It is your decision that determines your attitude, and attitude is everything.

STAND BY FAITH

The only currency that is legal tender in the Kingdom of God is faith. The Bible says:

By it the elders obtained a good report ... And these all, having obtained a good report through faith ...

Hebrews 11:2 and 39

Without faith, life is fake. But it takes no great faith to believe in things that can never fail, and God's Word abides forever. You must believe all that He has said about you and that it must and will be fulfilled.

Don't allow what you see with your natural eyes to rob you and reduce you to mediocrity. Remember: the One on the inside is more than conquerors, and He makes you *"more than conquerors"* too:

Nay, in all these things we are more than conquerors through him that loved us. Romans 8:37

That ye may be blameless and harmless, the sons of God, without rebuke, in the midst of a crooked and perverse nation, among whom ye shine as lights in the world. Philippians 2:15

*For it is God which worketh in you both
to will and to do of his good pleasure.*
                                    Philippians 2:13

There is no faith that fails to produce action. If you are to fulfill your mandate on the Earth, you must believe God and act in faith on His promises.

Like most believers, the disciples of Jesus felt the need for greater faith:

*And the apostles said unto the Lord,
Increase our faith. And the Lord said, If
ye had faith as a grain of mustard seed,
ye might say unto this sycamine tree,
Be thou plucked up by the root, and be
thou planted in the sea; and it should
obey you.*   Luke 17:5-6

Clearly, faith is activated by speaking out what you believe. Even when it looks silly, speak exactly what God has said. Speaking or declaring it leads to the needed action.

Ten lepers who were healed by Jesus were operating in faith:

And it came to pass, as he went to Jerusalem, that he passed through the midst of Samaria and Galilee. And as he entered into a certain village, there met him ten men that were lepers, which stood afar off: and they lifted up their voices, and said, Jesus, Master, have mercy on us.

And when he saw them, he said unto them, Go shew yourselves unto the priests. And it came to pass, that, as they went, they were cleansed.

And one of them, when he saw that he was healed, turned back, and with a loud voice glorified God, and fell down on his face at his feet, giving him thanks: and he was a Samaritan. And Jesus answering said, Were there not ten cleansed? but where are the nine? There are not found that returned to give glory to God, save this stranger. And he said unto him, Arise, go thy way: thy faith hath made thee whole

.   Luke 17:11-19

Why did these men leave? They were taking action. Jesus said they were healed, and the moment He said it, it was done. They believed it and acted on it. In the same way, put your faith to work. In doing this, you will surely fulfill your destiny. Activate it by declaring it and then living it out day by day.

You are *Destined for Greatness*, but there are things you must understand and put into practice in order to become outstanding.

CHAPTER 3

LEARNING TO LIVE IN GOD'S GLORY

In the sweat of thy face shalt thou eat bread, till thou return unto the ground; for out of it wast thou taken: for dust thou art, and unto dust shalt thou return.   Genesis 3:19

After the fall of Adam in the Garden of Eden, man lost his original design and was reduced from Elohim to mere dust. *"Dust thou art, and dust shalt thou return."* This was said to the same man who had been created in the image of God. The Spirit of God which had made him a supernatural being had now left him, and he became an ordinary being and a colossal failure to boot. Man was now subject to death, to nature, and to Satan's cunning.

The coming of Jesus Christ, thousands of years later, was to redeem us from Satan, forgive us of our sins, and heal us. It was also to produce many Jesuses on the Earth, those who would not live as a victim, as the first Adam had:

> *For it became him, for whom are all things, and by whom are all things, in bringing many sons unto glory, to make the captain of their salvation perfect through sufferings.* Hebrews 2:10

> *But ye are not in the flesh, but in the Spirit, if so be that the Spirit of God dwell in you. Now if any man have not the Spirit of Christ, he is none of his.*
> Romans 8:9

In Romans 6:5, Paul taught that we are now *"in the likeness of [Christ's] resurrection."* Never forget that Jesus Christ came to this

Earth, and when He did, He had preeminence over everything around Him:

> *For by Him all things were created that are in heaven and that are on earth, visible and invisible, whether thrones or dominions or principalities or powers. All things were created through Him and for Him. And He is before all things, and in Him all things consist. And He is the head of the body, the church, who is the beginning, the firstborn from the dead, that in all things He may have the preeminence.*
>
> Colossians 1:16-18, NKJV

We are now joint heirs with this divine preeminence through the outpouring of the Holy Spirit that is resident in us. What could be more amazing?

> *In Him you also trusted, after you heard the word of truth, the gospel of your salvation; in whom also, having believed, you were sealed with the Holy Spirit*

> *of promise, who is the guarantee of our inheritance until the redemption of the purchased possession, to the praise of His glory.* Ephesians 1:13, NKJV

There is a divine outpouring of God's power, God's life, and God's glory that comes into us at redemption. It makes us Christlike and fills us with the very omnipotency of God. This Spirit outpouring makes us immune to the onslaught of darkness and sets us far above anything that can be named. God's Spirit in us becomes a quickening force that will not permit death to reign over us:

> *But if the Spirit of Him who raised Jesus from the dead dwells in you, He who raised Christ from the dead will also give life to your mortal bodies through His Spirit who dwells in you.*
> Romans 8:11, NKJV

God needed the new creation believer to do His bidding on the Earth. The old man that we inherited from Adam could not withstand the forces of darkness and had no ability to carry this new level of glory that God wanted to send. *"Flesh and blood cannot inherit the kingdom of God"*:

> *Now this I say, brethren, that flesh and blood cannot inherit the kingdom of God; nor does corruption inherit incorruption.* 1 Corinthians 15:50, NKJV

In order to enter into the glory God has prepared for us, we need a total transformation, a totally new nature, and it cannot come by our own efforts. It is a work of His glorious grace:

> *But you are not in the flesh but in the Spirit, if indeed the Spirit of God dwells in you. Now if anyone does not have the Spirit of Christ, he is not His.*
> Romans 8:9, NKJV

> *There is no distinction, since all have sinned and continually fall short of*

the glory of God, and are being justi-
fied [declared free of the guilt of sin,
made acceptable to God, and granted
eternal life] as a gift by His [precious,
undeserved] grace, through the redemp-
tion [the payment for our sin] which is
[provided] in Christ Jesus.
Romans 3:23-24, AMP

It is this amazing grace that makes you a ruler over everything on the Earth, just as Jesus was when He walked here:

For if by one man's offence death reigned
by one; much more they which receive
abundance of grace and of the gift of
righteousness shall reign in life by one,
Jesus Christ. Romans 5:17

Grace becomes effectual when faith is re-leased to that end, for everything grace does is received by faith:

For the sin of this one man, Adam,
caused death to rule over many. But

even greater is God's wonderful grace and his gift of righteousness, for all who receive it will live in triumph over sin and death through this one man, Jesus Christ. Romans 5:17, NLT

By whom also we have access by faith into this grace wherein we stand, and rejoice in hope of the glory of God.
Romans 5:2

You don't have to do all the calisthenics. Grace brought you to the throne. It's amazing, but many don't believe it's true. The manifestation of God in us is called *"Christ in you, the hope of glory"* and you can't have Him in you and not show it if you believe it:

To whom God would make known what is the riches of the glory of this mystery among the Gentiles; which is Christ in you, the hope of glory. Colossians 1:27

According as his divine power hath given unto us all things that pertain unto

*life and godliness, through the knowl-
edge of him that hath called us to glory
and virtue: whereby are given unto us
exceeding great and precious promises:
that by these ye might be partakers of
the divine nature, having escaped the
corruption that is in the world through
lust.* 2 Peter 1:3-4

Grace brought us into glory. This is God coming down to our level to bring us to His level, and it happens without any human effort. It is employed by faith. God justifies you, declare you righteous, holy, and perfect, without you doing anything but believe. All the effort is His:

*Now to him that worketh is the reward not
reckoned of grace, but of debt. But to him
that worketh not, but believeth on him that
justifieth the ungodly, his faith is counted
for righteousness.* Romans 4:4-5

Beloved, Christ taking our place before God must not be underestimated. He is our

Substitution. He took our place in sin, in death, in sickness, and in poverty, and we are set free ... if and when we set our affections on Him.

How can God help you if you doubt His Word? He said, *"He that believe not shall be dammed":*

> *He that believeth and is baptized shall be saved; but he that believeth not shall be damned.* Mark 16:16

It was the grace of God that took away all limits and restored to us the glory lost in Adam's time. Paul preached at Antioch:

> *Men and brethren, children of the stock of Abraham, and whosoever among you feareth God, to you is the word of this salvation sent. For they that dwell at Jerusalem, and their rulers, because they knew him not, nor yet the voices of the prophets which are read every sabbath day, they have fulfilled them in condemning him. And though they*

73

found no cause of death in him, yet desired they Pilate that he should be slain. And when they had fulfilled all that was written of him, they took him down from the tree, and laid him in a sepulchre. But God raised him from the dead: and he was seen many days of them which came up with him from Galilee to Jerusalem, who are his witnesses unto the people.

And we declare unto you glad tidings, how that the promise which was made unto the fathers, God hath fulfilled the same unto us their children, in that he hath raised up Jesus again; as it is also written in the second psalm, Thou art my Son, this day have I begotten thee.

And as concerning that he raised him up from the dead, now no more to return to corruption, he said on this wise, I will give you the sure mercies of David.

Wherefore he saith also in another psalm, Thou shalt not suffer thine Holy One to see corruption.

For David, after he had served his own generation by the will of God, fell on *sleep, and was laid unto his fathers, and saw corruption: but he, whom God raised again, saw no corruption.*

Be it known unto you therefore, men and brethren, that through this man is preached unto you the forgiveness of sins: and by him all that believe are justified from all things, from which ye could not be justified by the law of Moses. Beware therefore, lest that come upon you, which is spoken of in the prophets;

Behold, ye despisers, and wonder, and perish: for I work a work in your days, a work which ye shall in no wise believe, though a man declare it unto you.

Acts 13:26-41

He was preaching about sonship. You and I are now the beloved of God, and we have *"the sure mercies of David."* The world may not like us, but God chose us, and that's all that counts. What has not worked for others will work for us. We experience mercies beyond our faith because of Jesus.

75

Our enemies become helpers of our dream, all because of the mercies of God. We saw this fulfilled in Christ, and by His grace it can be our testimony too. No more corruption if you believe.

Notice what happened in this passage:

> They were ware of it, and fled unto Lystra and Derbe, cities of Lycaonia, and unto the region that lieth round about: and there they preached the gospel.
> And there sat a certain man at Lystra, impotent in his feet, being a cripple from his mother's womb, who never had walked: the same heard Paul speak: who stedfastly beholding him, and perceiving that he had faith to be healed, said with a loud voice, Stand upright on thy feet. And he leaped and walked.
>
> Acts 14:6-10

These disciples were hated and mistreated and forced to flee, but then miracles started happening. It was no more what they did; it was based on what Jesus had done and their faith in Him. Do you believe?

There were two Adams and both of them led a generation. One led a generation to death and bondage, and the other led a generation to life and glory:

> *And so it is written, The first man Adam was made a living soul; the last Adam was made a quickening spirit.*
>
> 1 Corinthians 15:45

You have belonged to the first Adam, but you must disconnect yourself from him. If not, you will know nothing but sickness, disease, and death. Get connected to the Last Adam, Jesus Christ:

> *Wherefore, as by one man sin entered into the world, and death by sin; and so death passed upon all men, for that all have sinned:*
> *For as by one man's disobedience many were made sinners, so by the obedience of one shall many be made righteous.*

77

> *Moreover the law entered, that the offence might abound. But where sin abounded, grace did much more abound.*
>
> Romans 5:12 and 19-20

Through the Last Adam, we become new and are reconnected to God's glory. Now we have the Good News, the Gospel, and are no longer subject to oppression and weakness. Instead, we are *"strong in the Lord, and in the power of his might"* (Ephesians 6:10). It is very difficult to understand this if the Spirit of God is not revealing it to you:

> *That the God of our Lord Jesus Christ, the Father of glory, may give unto you the spirit of wisdom and revelation in the knowledge of him: the eyes of your understanding being enlightened; that ye may know what is the hope of his calling, and what the riches of the glory of his inheritance in the saints, and what is the exceeding greatness of his power to us-ward who believe, according to the working of his mighty power, which he*

wrought in Christ, when he raised him from the dead, and set him at his own right hand in the heavenly places, far above all principality, and power, and might, and dominion, and every name that is named, not only in this world, but also in that which is to come. Ephesians 1:17-21

God *"wrought,"* or performed, this when He raised Christ from the dead. The result is that something separates you and takes you completely out from under the reach of darkness and puts you in charge:

> *Who hath delivered us from the power of darkness, and hath translated us into the kingdom of his dear Son.*
> Colossians 1:13

The grace we have received has connected us to what is required in order for us to take over, and that is true righteousness:

> *For if by one man's offence death reigned by one; much more they which receive*

> *abundance of grace and of the gift of*
> *righteousness shall reign in life by one,*
> *Jesus Christ.*   Romans 5:17

What is righteousness? It is the ability to have a right standing before God, to stand before Him with no guilt, no fear, and no condemnation. And it is all done on God's account. You can stand before God as if sin had never existed in you.

Never forget that fear and intimidation only came to man when he had sinned. Adam said to God, *"I heard Your voice in the garden, and I was afraid, ... and I hid myself"* (Genesis 3:10). " Contrast that with the righteousness boldness that is ours through Christ:

> *Let us therefore come boldly unto the*
> *throne of grace, that we may obtain*
> *mercy, and find grace to help in time of*
> *need.*   Hebrews 4:16

God wants you to know your present po-sition. You are now coequal with God the

Father, Son, and Holy Spirit by His grace. He said:

> *Whose soever sins ye remit, they are remitted unto them; and whose soever sins ye retain, they are retained.*
>
> John 20:23

That sounds very odd, but it's the truth. Jesus also said, *"That they may be one, even as we [God the Father, Jesus, and the Holy Spirit] are one":*

> *And the glory which thou gavest me I have given them; that they may be one, even as we are one: I in them, and thou in me, that they may be made perfect in one; and that the world may know that thou hast sent me, and hast loved them, as thou hast loved me.*   John 17:22-23

We now have the authority to remove a person from the dungeons of darkness, to free them from sickness and disease, and to place them in the plan of God for eternity.

When Paul was opposed by a sorcerer in Paphos, a city in Cyprus, he did something very unusual:

> *Then Saul, who also is called Paul, filled with the Holy Spirit, looked intently at him and said, "O full of all deceit and all fraud, you son of the devil, you enemy of all righteousness, will you not cease perverting the straight ways of the Lord? And now, indeed, the hand of the Lord is upon you, and you shall be blind, not seeing the sun for a time." And immediately a dark mist fell on him, and he went around seeking someone to lead him by the hand.* Acts 13:9-11, NKJV

No matter how much or how often Satan tries to hurt and frustrate you, God is closer to you than Satan. Our God is *"a very present help"* in times of trouble:

> *God is our refuge and strength, A very present help in trouble.*
> Psalm 46:1, NKJV

God has said of His people:

Behold, the days come, saith the LORD, that I will raise unto David a righteous Branch, and a King shall reign and prosper, and shall execute judgment and justice in the earth. In his days Judah shall be saved, and Israel shall dwell safely: and this is his name whereby he shall be called, The LORD Our Righteousness.

Therefore, behold, the days come, saith the LORD, that they shall no more say, The LORD liveth, which brought up the children of Israel out of the land of Egypt; but, The LORD liveth, which brought up and which led the seed of the house of Israel out of the north country, and from all countries whither I had driven them; and they shall dwell in their own land. Mine heart within me is broken because of the prophets; all my bones shake; I am like a drunken man, and like a man whom wine hath overcome, because of

the LORD, *and because of the words of*
his holiness. Jeremiah 23:5-9

You get everything for nothing by grace through faith. Jesus said:

Is anyone thirsty? Come and drink-
even if you have no money! Come, take
your choice of wine or milk—it's all
free! Isaiah 55:1, NLT

That, my friend, is grace in action.

On the basis of God's promises, declare in prayer today:

1. Father, in the name of Jesus Christ, I have the right to be wealthy, blessed, and healed, and to live a long life because I have access to the throne through Jesus Christ. I receive it now in Jesus' name.

2. Father, on the basis of Your promises, I reject sorrow, pain, and affliction now in Jesus' name.

Now act on it.

God's glory comes to us in levels, and you determine the level you want to operate in by your exposure to knowledge and your application of the truth. Paul wrote:

> *But we all, with open face beholding as in a glass the glory of the Lord, are changed into the same image from glory to glory, even as by the Spirit of the Lord.* 2 Corinthians 3:18

> *For God, who commanded the light to shine out of darkness, hath shined in our hearts, to give the light of the knowledge of the glory of God in the face of Jesus Christ.* 2 Corinthians 4:6

God's glory manifests through knowledge. You must know, for instance, that we believers were sent here to dominate the Earth. That is our calling. But without financial provision, dominion is questioned, and glory has the appearance of being fake. Adam and Eve believed in and manifested their dominion, and it was obvious to all that they were blessed:

> *And God blessed them [granting them certain authority] and said to them, "Be fruitful, multiply, and fill the earth, and subjugate it [putting it under your power]; and rule over (dominate) the fish of the sea, the birds of the air, and every living thing that moves upon the earth."*   Genesis 1:28, AMP

Without material possessions, the glory on our lives is incomplete. Let God bless you.

The first time glory was mentioned in the Bible it was in reference to wealth:

> *And he heard the words of Laban's sons, saying, Jacob hath taken away all that was our father's; and of that which was our father's hath he gotten all this glory.*
> Genesis 31:1

The fact that we are created for God's glory means that we are created for blessing,

and that includes financial wealth, even
though it's more than money:

> *Everyone who is called by My Name,*
> *Whom I have created for My glory,*
> *Whom I have formed, even whom I have*
> *made.*   Isaiah 43:7, AMP

The world does not have answers to the
blessing issue, but God does. True blessing
is free of sorrow:

> *The blessing of the* LORD *brings [true]*
> *riches,*
> *And He adds no sorrow to it [for it*
> *comes as a blessing from God].*
>   Proverbs 10:22, AMP

God reveals secrets to His children, and
He expects us to walk in obedience to
the truth He reveals. He took Abraham
out of the world system in order to make
him an institution on the Earth. He said
to him:

"Go away from your country,
And from your relatives
And from your father's house,
To the land which I will show you;
And I will make you a great nation,
And I will bless you [abundantly],
And make your name great (exalted,
distinguished);
And you shall be a blessing [a source of
great good to others].

Genesis 12:1-2, AMP

The world cannot make you financially free without putting you under pressure and without you facing conditions and burdens. In the world, you are made to bow to something that is not God.

God, however, is a supernatural God, and when we connect with Him in a supernatural way, He supplies all our needs in a supernatural way. The Holy Ghost came into this world and into God's children with the manifestation of abundance. Joel records:

"And I will compensate you for the years
That the swarming locust has eaten,
The creeping locust, the stripping locust,
and the gnawing locust—
My great army which I sent among you.
You will have plenty to eat and be satisfied
And praise the name of the LORD *your*
God
Who has dealt wondrously with you;
And My people shall never be put to
shame.
And you shall know [without any
doubt] that I am in the midst of Israel
[to protect and bless you],
And that I am the LORD *your God,*
And there is no other;
My people will never be put to shame.
It shall come about after this
That I shall pour out My Spirit on all
mankind;
And your sons and your daughters will
prophesy,
Your old men will dream dreams,
Your young men will see visions."

                              Joel 2:25-28, AMP

We are not and must not be ambassadors of failure, poverty, and lack. We are ambassadors of Christ, and Christ is everything mankind will ever need. There is no one who is in Christ who cannot live in abundance, and that means you ... if you are willing to walk in covenant with God (see Genesis 12:1-20).

God had you and me in mind when He was giving the covenant blessing to Abraham. To enter the realm of wealth, you need to know and believe that it is yours by covenant through God's Spirit that dwells in you.

That fact alone puts every limitation, failure, and lack under your feet. What God poured into Abraham can now come to you. It is called covenant blessing:

> *Now to Abraham and his seed were the promises made. He saith not, And to seeds, as of many; but as of one, And to thy seed, which is Christ.*
> *And if ye be Christ's, then are ye Abraham's seed, and heirs according to the promise.* Galatians 3:16 and 29

Thus saith the LORD to his anointed, to Cyrus, whose right hand I have holden, to subdue nations before him; and I will loose the loins of kings, to open before him the two leaved gates; and the gates shall not be shut; I will go before thee, and make the crooked places straight: I will break in pieces the gates of brass, and cut in sunder the bars of iron: and I will give thee the treasures of darkness, and hidden riches of secret places, that thou mayest know that I, the LORD, which call thee by thy name, am the God of Israel.   Isaiah 45:1-3

In Christ, you are authorized to subdue, to loose, and to open. Start subduing, loosing, and opening. God removes the gates, so be expecting a flood of wealth in the days to come.

You are *Destined for Greatness*, but there are things you must understand and put into practice in order to become outstanding.

CHAPTER 4

WHAT TO KNOW

And ye shall know the truth, and the truth shall make you free. John 8:32

STICK TO THE TRUTH, NO MATTER WHAT

The major enemy of the truth is distraction. If you will stick to the truth, you will experience freedom. People who don't have truth themselves cannot teach you. They will only confuse you. Above all, stick with what God has said until you experience it for yourself. And never lose sight of truth or those who possess it, and adhere to their instructions. Ruth of old learned this lesson well:

And they lifted up their voice, and wept again: and Orpah kissed her mother in law; but Ruth clave unto her. And she said, Behold, thy sister in law is gone back unto her people, and unto her gods: return thou after thy sister in law.

And Ruth said, Intreat me not to leave thee, or to return from following after thee: for whither thou goest, I will go; and where thou lodgest, I will lodge: thy people shall be my people, and thy God my God: where thou diest, will I die, and there will I be buried: the LORD do so to me, and more also, if ought but death part thee and me.

When she saw that she was stedfastly minded to go with her, then she left speaking unto her. Ruth 1:14-18

Ruth saw something in Naomi that impressed her. In her mother-in-law, she saw covenant and a future. At the moment, both women were in a desperate situation, and, to the natural eye, the future looked bleak. But somehow Naomi knew there was a future for them in God's covenant, and Ruth caught that faith. At the moment, she was a cursed Moabite, but she was about to change the story. In time, she married Boaz and owned everything.

Another example of someone who insisted on staying close to a person of faith and truth was Elisha.

ELIJAH AND ELISHA

And it came to pass, when the LORD would take up Elijah into heaven by a whirlwind, that Elijah went with Elisha from Gilgal. And Elijah said unto Elisha, Tarry here, I pray thee; for the Lord hath sent me to Bethel. And Elisha said unto him, As the LORD liveth, and as thy soul liveth, I will not leave thee. So they went down to Bethel.

2 Kings 2:1-2

Your miracle may take some time, but don't give up quickly. Stick close to people of faith and truth until you get what God has promised.

95

In the morning sow thy seed, and in the evening withhold not thine hand: for thou knowest not whether shall prosper, either this or that, or whether they both shall be alike good. Ecclesiastes 11:6

Your time is coming. Wait patiently in faith.

KNOW THE SOURCE, AND YOU WILL CHANGE YOUR STATUS

Many claim God as the Owner and Creator of the Universe, but few see Him as Daddy, the Source for their lives. If God is Daddy (and He is), then your needs are all met. Every fear dies when you know that God owns it all, and He is your Source. If your business or job is your source, you may wake up every morning in fear of what might happen. You may suffer as long as you don't know Who God is to you. The moment you know Him as your Source, you change your whole way of thinking:

Blessed is the man that trusteth in the Lord, and whose hope the Lord is. For he shall be as a tree planted by the waters, and that spreadeth out her roots by the river, and shall not see when heat cometh, but her leaf shall be green; and shall not be careful in the year of drought, neither shall cease from yielding fruit. Jeremiah 17:7-8

Preceding these wonderful promises came the curses:

Thus saith the Lord; Cursed be the man that trusteth in man, and maketh flesh his arm, and whose heart departeth from the Lord. For he shall be like the heath in the desert, and shall not see when good cometh; but shall inhabit the parched places in the wilderness, in a salt land and not inhabited. Jeremiah 17:5-6

Which will it be for you, blessings or curses?

JOSEPH AND HIS BROTHERS

Another great biblical example of people sticking with persons of faith and truth is of Joseph and his brothers. Joseph discovered God's truth long before his brothers, and although they hated him, he prospered, and they suffered famine:

> *Then Joseph commanded to fill their sacks with corn, and to restore every man's money into his sack, and to give them provision for the way: and thus did he unto them.* Genesis 42:25

> *And he commanded the steward of his house, saying, Fill the men's sacks with food, as much as they can carry, and put every man's money in his sack's mouth.* Genesis 44:1

> *Now thou art commanded, this do ye; take you wagons out of the land of Egypt for your little ones, and for your wives, and bring your father, and come. And*

the children of Israel did so: and Joseph gave them wagons, according to the commandment of Pharaoh, and gave them provision for the way.

And they [Joseph's brothers] told him [Jacob, their father] all the words of Joseph, which he had said unto them: and when he saw the wagons which Joseph had sent to carry him, the spirit of Jacob their father revived.

Genesis 45:19, 21 and 27

Your Brother, the Firstborn, Jesus, is in charge of Heaven's storehouse, so you must hear His truthful words and follow Him faithfully.

USE WHAT HAS BEEN GIVEN TO YOU

A scepter of wealth has been given to you to overcome lack and poverty, but, like so many, you may not have used it yet:

And God said, Let us make man in our image, after our likeness: and let them have

99

dominion over the fish of the sea, and over the fowl of the air, and over the cattle, and over all the earth, and over every creeping thing that creepeth upon the earth.

And God blessed them, and God said unto them, Be fruitful, and multiply, and replenish the earth, and subdue it: and have dominion over the fish of the sea, and over the fowl of the air, and over every living thing that moveth upon the earth. Genesis 1:26 and 28

And I beheld, and I heard the voice of many angels round about the throne and the beasts and the elders: and the number of them was ten thousand times ten thousand, and thousands of thousands; saying with a loud voice, Worthy is the Lamb that was slain to receive power, and riches, and wisdom, and strength, and honour, and glory, and blessing. Revelation 5:11-12

"Power, and riches, and wisdom, and strength, and honour, and glory." And you are Christ's heir.

What the enemy excels in is bringing to us imaginations that are contrary to the mind of God, and in this way he is able to bring many into bondage. Your heavenly imagination reveals the "I AM" gene and the traits of God in you. You can have all that God has because you are a joint heir with Christ. Stop entertaining Satan's vain imaginations. Build up your heavenly imagination by faith through the Word of God. It can give you a clear picture of your future. And it's all a gift from God. It is also your calling. See in the Spirit the picture of what God puts before you. See as He sees:

> *And God said, Let us make man in our image, after our likeness: and let them have dominion over the fish of the sea, and over the fowl of the air, and over the cattle, and over all the earth, and over every creeping thing that creepeth upon the earth.* Genesis 1:26

You are over the Earth, not subject to the Earth. God said it. Man "messed up," but the Second Adam picked up the pieces and put them together again. He dominated, just like the first Adam before the Fall, and gave us back dominion over the Earth, and this includes over the wealth of the Earth.

But you can't understand dominion until you understand the power of a seed:

> *And God blessed them, and God said unto them, Be fruitful, and multiply, and replenish the earth, and subdue it: and have dominion over the fish of the sea, and over the fowl of the air, and over every living thing that moveth upon the earth. And God said, Behold, I have given you every herb bearing seed, which is upon the face of all the earth, and every tree, in the which is the fruit of a tree yielding seed; to you it shall be for meat.*
>
> *And to every beast of the earth, and to every fowl of the air, and to every thing that creepeth upon the earth, wherein there is life, I have given every green herb for meat: and it was so. And God*

saw every thing that he had made, and,
behold, it was very good. And the eve-
ning and the morning were the sixth
day. Genesis 1:28-31

You cannot command wealth if you don't
know you are a commander, a commander
through your seed. God wants you to dominate in the area of wealth, as in everything
else:

The heaven, even the heavens, are the
Lord's: but the earth hath he given to
the children of men. Psalm 115:16

This is a commission, not a confession:

For the land, whither thou goest in to
possess it, is not as the land of Egypt,
from whence ye came out, where thou
sowedst thy seed, and wateredst it with
thy foot, as a garden of herbs: but the
land, whither ye go to possess it, is a
land of hills and valleys, and drinketh
water of the rain of heaven: a land which

> *the LORD thy God careth for: the eyes of*
> *the LORD thy God are always upon it,*
> *from the beginning of the year even unto*
> *the end of the year.*
> Deuteronomy 11:10-12

We become rulers by our giving, not by our confession. The test of your faithfulness is in your commitment to your giving. This requires actions, not just words.

Because you are created in the image of God, you have the identity of God in you to create waves. Jesus said:

> *He that hath seen me hath seen the*
> *Father.* John 14:9

And that should be your testimony too. We who call ourselves believers talk too much in church and don't act nearly enough. We have the power to be wealthy, so we need to use it:.

> *But thou shalt remember the LORD thy*
> *God: for it is he that giveth thee power*

to get wealth, that he may establish his covenant which he sware unto thy fathers, as it is this day.

Deuteronomy 8:18

This *"power to get wealth"* is release upon you now in Jesus' name. Paul wrote:

Now unto him that is able to do exceeding abundantly above all that we ask or think, according to the power that worketh in us. Ephesians 3:20

Command the wealth to manifest in your life now:

Thus saith the LORD, the Holy One of Israel, and his Maker, Ask me of things to come concerning my sons, and concerning the work of my hands command ye me. Isaiah 45:11

If we know that Jesus is the Lord over everything, we can then use His name to get all that we need. Pray believing prayers such as:

1. Father, in the name of Jesus Christ, I take my territory now in Jesus' name.

2. Father, in the name of Jesus Christ, I decree: money, wealth, hear me and come to me now in Jesus' name.

3. Father, in the name of Jesus Christ, I decree mighty and strange ideas. Opportunities beyond human calculation, come now in Jesus' name.

4. From henceforth I will drink the rain of Heaven. No more stagnation in the name of Jesus.

You cannot be made in the image and likeness of God and be a failure, Never! You cannot carry the Spirit of God in you and not have His glory upon you. Never!

And God said, Let us make man in our image, after our likeness: and let them have dominion over the fish of the sea, and over the fowl of the air, and over the

cattle, and over all the earth, and over
every creeping thing that creepeth upon
the earth.   Genesis 1:26

This puts you in an envied class among all
of creation, include other men and women.
Never forget: all things were put under you
by God Himself, and you therefore have
the authority to call them when they are
needed by applying the principles of God's
Kingdom.

The psalmist declared:

When I consider thy heavens, the work
of thy fingers, the moon and the stars,
which thou hast ordained; what is man,
that thou art mindful of him? and the
son of man, that thou visitest him? For
thou hast made him a little lower than
the angels, and hast crowned him with
glory and honour. Thou madest him to
have dominion over the works of thy
hands; thou hast put all things under
his feet.   Psalm 8:3-6

>   *Thus saith the LORD, the Holy One of Israel, and his Maker, Ask me of things to come concerning my sons, and concerning the work of my hands command ye me.*   Isaiah 45:11

Every Kingdom citizen is destined to shine. Why? Because they are a reflection of the glory of God. All it takes is for them to rise and refuse to be intimidated by the forces of darkness that want to stop them. God called:

>   *"Arise, Jerusalem! Let your light shine for all to see.*
>   *For the glory of the LORD rises to shine on you.*
>   *Darkness as black as night covers all the nations of the earth,*
>   *but the glory of the LORD rises and appears over you.*
>   *All nations will come to your light; mighty kings will come to see your radiance."*   Isaiah 60:1-3, NLT

You are beyond reproach because your light shines forth, and darkness cannot snuff it out. God is not saying there will be no dark times; He is saying that when dark times come, you can handle them:

> *You are the light of the world. A city that is set on a hill cannot be hidden.*
> Matthew 5:14

This was spoken by the Owner of the Universe, so what's your problem? Where there is no light, men will be compelled to come to *your* light. Because of that, in the days ahead, you will excel in and through the name of Jesus Christ.

Instead of going to the world to learn the rudiments of life, let us go to God Himself. He will teach us His ways, and that is what will make the Church of Jesus Christ extraordinary:

> *Now it shall come to pass in the latter days*
> *That the mountain of the LORD's house*
> *Shall be established on the top of the mountains,*

> *And shall be exalted above the hills;*
> *And all nations shall flow to it.*
> *Many people shall come and say,*
> *"Come, and let us go up to the mountain*
> *of the* LORD,
> *To the house of the God of Jacob;*
> *He will teach us His ways,*
> *And we shall walk in His paths."*
> *For out of Zion shall go forth the law,*
> *And the word of the* LORD *from*
> *Jerusalem.*   Isaiah 2:2-3, NKJV

You are *Destined for Greatness,* but there are things you must understand and put into practice in order to become outstanding.

CHAPTER 5

WHAT TO DO WHEN THINGS SEEM TO BE GOING WRONG

Declaring the end from the beginning, and from ancient times the things that are not yet done, saying, My counsel shall stand, and I will do all my pleasure. Isaiah 46:10

HAVE AN UNWAVERING FOCUS

When success fails, focus should be questioned. Never forget that God finished the journey before calling you into it, and His plans never fail. It is lack of focus that derails people. Man was created to achieve whatever he focuses on, whatever he puts his mind to. Jesus said:

> *The light of the body is the eye: if therefore thine eye be single, thy whole body shall be full of light.* Matthew 6:22

> *Ye are the light of the world. A city that is set on an hill cannot be hid.*
>
> Matthew 5:14

You become whatever you focus on. Why? Focus increases your energy to achieve and perform. Focus eliminates distractions.

There is a part of the human brain called the prefrontal cortex or inferior frontal cortex (IFJ). This portion of your brain maintains a picture of your goals. As far as your brain is concerned, what you are focusing on is as good as done. The Bible knew this before science discovered it:

> *For the LORD God will help me; therefore shall I not be confounded: therefore have*

I set my face like a flint, and I know that
I shall not be ashamed.   Isaiah 50:7

When you are focused, you release the power of God to get the job done for you. If you lack focus, you will forever remain a victim. Focus defeats all doubts.

USE THE PRINCIPLE OF IMAGINATION

One of the greatest gifts God has given to man, one which no power can defeat, is the gift of imagination. There is a camera in your mind that takes a picture of your future and replays it to you for your action. That brings your future into the present:

> *And the LORD said, Behold, the people is*
> *one, and they have all one language; and*
> *this they begin to do: and now nothing*
> *will be restrained from them, which they*
> *have imagined to do.*   Genesis 11:6

That was imagination. Imagination enabled David to kill Goliath. He had

113

experienced God's help in killing a lion and a bear with his bare hands, and he, therefore, concluded, "This giants has to go." All of us have this gift of imagination; the problem is the enemy perverts it and uses it to his advantage:

> *For though we walk in the flesh, we do not war according to the flesh. For the weapons of our warfare are not carnal but mighty in God for pulling down strongholds, casting down arguments and every high thing that exalts itself against the knowledge of God, bringing every thought into captivity to the obedience of Christ.*
> 2 Corinthians 10:3-5, NKJV

Often, when you watch a movie, you become very emotionally involved. You are brought to tears or frightened. But those people on the screen are just acting, and you knew that before you started watching. You know that what you're seeing isn't real, and yet your mind is playing tricks on you. It suddenly seems very real indeed.

Your future success is first revealed in your mind, your imagination. If you believe what God is showing you, you won't worry about how you will achieve this image. God will take you there if you accept the image He puts in your imagination. Believe it and act on it.

SET YOUR GOALS BASED ON YOUR RIGHTEOUS DESIRES

God gives us desires, and when those desires come, they are like a tree of life:

> *You grew weary in your search, but you never gave up. Desire gave you renewed strength, and you did not grow weary.*
> Isaiah 57:10, NLT

But having dreams without a set goal in mind is like having a house with no foundation. You might need to write down what God is showing you. Write down what you want on one page, and write what you don't want on another. Write down the time frame in which you believe God will give it to you. Then, use those pages as a meaningful guide to prayer.

Pray in the Holy Ghost over your plan, and be sensitive to who God is sending your way to confirm your dreams. There are gifted dream interpreters in the Body of Christ, and God will send one to you if you will not despise them.

PLAN AHEAD

Pray about what can be done to achieve the first five things on your list. That is called planning. It is not carnal. Do it in the Spirit. This may require that you read books and get ideas from other people. Their advice will further fuel the dream God has put in your heart.

BE DISCIPLINED AND TAKE RESPONSIBILITY

Whatever you despise you cannot attract. Never forget this: God gives you grace, but you give yourself discipline. There are no heights to which you cannot go if you are willing to discipline yourself. But God will not read for you, nor attend seminars, nor go to classes for you. That's all your responsibility. Be wise:

> *A wise man will hear, and will increase learning; and a man of understanding shall attain unto wise counsels.*
>
> Proverbs 1:5

> *For wisdom is a defence, and money is a defence: but the excellency of knowledge is, that wisdom giveth life to them that have it.* Ecclesiastes 7:12

When you have looked at what it will take to fulfill your dream, start taking action. Give whatever it takes, always depending on the grace of God.

GIVE GOD THANKS

If and when you decide to depend on yourself totally, you will make a mess of things. Giving God thanks releases His ability into your life to experience Heaven on Earth. Paul wrote:

> *In every thing give thanks: for this is the will of God in Christ Jesus concerning you.* 1 Thessalonians 5:18

The psalmist wrote:

> *Let the people praise thee, O God; let all the people praise thee. Then shall the earth yield her increase; and God, even our own God, shall bless us. God shall bless us; and all the ends of the earth shall fear him.* Psalm 67:5-7

It takes revelation of the Word to become a legend in the Kingdom.

> *Open thou mine eyes, that I may behold wondrous things out of thy law.*
> Psalm 119:18

They know not, neither will they understand; they walk on in darkness: all the foundations of the earth are out of course. I have said, Ye are gods; and all of you are children of the most High. But ye shall die like men, and fall like one of the princes.   Psalm 82:5-7

God's people were not intended to die like other men, but they didn't know that. The Word of God is full of wonder, and when you believe it, the manifestation is beyond human comprehension.

UNDERSTAND THE MINISTRY OF ANGELS AS IT RELATES TO YOUR GREATNESS

Every child of God has a Canaan's Land, a destination, a glory, but between you and that destination, there are giants, there is a Jordan, and there are Amalekites, and they all want to stop you from rising. Sickness and demons are your enemies, but your Father has given you provision to stop the mouths of the adversaries. He has also given us His angels:

> *Behold, I send an Angel before thee, to keep thee in the way, and to bring thee into the place which I have prepared. Beware of him, and obey his voice, provoke him not; for he will not pardon your transgressions: for my name is in him.* Exodus 23:20-21

Angels are supernatural beings that cannot be stopped by men or by any other means. Psalm 103:20 says they *"excel in strength."*

> *Bless the LORD, ye his angels, that excel in strength, that do his commandments, hearkening unto the voice of his word.*

The name of the Lord is in His holy angels. Every covenant person in the Bible had angelic assistance to get to their place of glory. Abraham, for instance, believed deeply in the ministry of angels, and God showed him this was the key to the manifestation of his dream:

> *The LORD God of heaven, which took me from my father's house, and from the land of my kindred, and which spake unto me, and that sware unto me, saying, Unto thy seed will I give this land; he shall send his angel before thee, and thou shalt take a wife unto my son from thence.*
> *And he [Eleazar] said, I am Abraham's servant. And the LORD hath blessed my master greatly; and he is become great: and he hath given him flocks, and herds, and silver, and gold, and menservants, and maidservants, and camels, and asses.*   Genesis 24:7 and 34-35

Angels do things that are, for us humans, out of the ordinary, and the good news is that every child of God has angels that follow them everywhere they go:

> *The angel of the LORD encampeth round about them that fear him, and delivereth them.*   Psalm 34:7

121

*"The angel of the L*ORD *encamps"* round about you too, and you can activate these heavenly beings by acknowledging their presence and by speaking the Word of God by faith. Angels don't follow feelings; they only obey God's Word.

We were intended to operate in the Spirit, bringing the invisible world into reality, making the physical world obey us. The impossible becomes possible when we operate in the supernatural, controlling things by the force of the Spirit.

As we operate in the invisible realm, what we are believing for and declaring starts to manifest in the physical realm. This is based on action, not feeling, It is caused by trust and dependency on the realm of the Spirit based upon the Word of God.

Angels are agents of Heaven that nobody can stop, and as noted, the Bible says they *"excel in strength."* Angels accompanied and aided Abraham's servant in Old Testament times:

And he said unto me, The LORD, before whom I walk, will send his angel with thee, and prosper thy way; and thou shalt take a wife for my son of my kindred, and of my father's house.

Genesis 24:40

Angels are available to do the same for us now in New Testament times:

Are they not all ministering spirits, sent forth to minister for them who shall be heirs of salvation? Hebrews 1:14

You don't need to help the Scriptures. Let the Lord say what He means. He does it well.

Angels minister *for* you, meaning they don't need your assistance; they just need your belief, the exercise of your faith. If angels brought the good news of the conception of Jesus, they can get you whatever you need from God today.

Mary was talking to an angel, and you can talk to angels too. The angel that spoke to

Mary departed once it was apparent that she believed and received the message, and your dream is coming to pass too in Jesus' name.

The invisible world stops working when you look to man, and not to God. Mary said to the angel, *"I know not a man"*:

And in the sixth month the angel Gabriel was sent from God unto a city of Galilee, named Nazareth, to a virgin espoused to a man whose name was Joseph, of the house of David; and the virgin's name was Mary. And the angel came in unto her, and said, Hail, thou that art highly favoured, the Lord is with thee: blessed art thou among women. And when she saw him, she was troubled at his saying, and cast in her mind what manner of salutation this should be. And the angel said unto her, Fear not, Mary: for thou hast found favour with God. And, behold, thou shalt conceive in thy womb, and bring forth a son, and shalt call his name Jesus. He shall be great, and shall be called the Son of the Highest: and the Lord God shall give unto him the throne of his father David: and he shall reign over the house of Jacob for ever; and of his kingdom there shall be no end.

Then said Mary unto the angel, How shall this be, seeing I know not a man? And the angel answered and said unto her, The Holy Ghost shall come upon thee, and the power of the Highest shall overshadow thee: therefore also that holy thing which shall be born of thee shall be called the Son of God. And, behold, thy cousin Elisabeth, she hath also conceived a son in her old age: and this is the sixth month with her, who was called barren. For with God nothing shall be impossible. Luke 1:26-37

Angels work with the Holy Ghost, and the full potential of the Spirit is expressed by angels and their activities on our behalf:

After this there was a feast of the Jews; and Jesus went up to Jerusalem. Now

125

there is at Jerusalem by the sheep market a pool, which is called in the Hebrew tongue Bethesda, having five porches. In these lay a great multitude of impotent folk, of blind, halt, withered, waiting for the moving of the water. For an angel went down at a certain season into the pool, and troubled the water: whosoever then first after the troubling of the water stepped in was made whole of whatsoever disease he had.   John 5:1-4

There is another stirring going on right now. Your deliverance is here, and you will be made whole. Believe and receive!

An angel saved Daniel by shutting the mouths of the lions:

And when he came to the den, he cried with a lamentable voice unto Daniel: and the king spake and said to Daniel, O Daniel, servant of the living God, is thy God, whom thou servest continually, able to deliver thee from the lions? Then said Daniel unto the king, O king, live for ever. My God hath sent his angel, and hath shut the lions' mouths, that they have not hurt me: forasmuch as before him innocency was found in me; and also before thee, O king, have I done no hurt. Daniel 6:20-22

Angels ministered to Jesus:

And he was there in the wilderness forty days, tempted of Satan; and was with the wild beasts; and the angels ministered unto him. Mark 1:13

Dominating the Earth would not be possible without supernatural enthronement. We can command the Universe because God, the Creator, has given unto us *"all things that pertain to life and godliness"*:

According as his divine power hath given unto us all things that pertain unto life and godliness, through the knowledge of him that hath called us to glory and virtue. 2 Peter 1:3

The ministry of angels is key to our rulership and glory here on the Earth. When you recognize this provision God has made, and you engage it by faith, you cannot be denied. The strength and the ability of the angels makes their ministry unstoppable by men and/or any other force. Again:

> Bless the LORD, ye his angels, that excel
> in strength, that do his commandments,
> hearkening unto the voice of his word.
> Psalm 103:20

This means that some of our redemptive benefits cannot be obtained without the assistance of angels. There are victories that would be aborted without them.

The angel of the Lord came between the children of Israel and the Egyptians and appeared in the pillar of cloud by day and the pillar of fire by night:

> And the angel of God, which went before
> the camp of Israel, removed and went
> behind them; and the pillar of the cloud

went from before their face, and stood
behind them.   Exodus 14:19

In fact, God showed Moses that taking
the Promised Land would not be possible
without the ministry of angels:

Behold, I send an Angel before thee, to
keep thee in the way, and to bring thee
into the place which I have prepared.
                                   Exodus 23:20

The fiery strength of God's angelic hosts
with us today is the reason we cannot be
stopped; they guard us and guide us to our
God-given destiny in Christ.

Nobody in the Body of Christ was destined to be a victim. There are armies of
angels released from Heaven to attend to
our journey in life. The Bible says, *"They will*
carry you in their arms lest you dash your feet
against a stone":

There shall no evil befall thee, nei-
ther shall any plague come nigh thy

dwelling. For he shall give his angels charge over thee, to keep thee in all thy ways. They shall bear thee up in their hands, lest thou dash thy foot against a stone. Thou shalt tread upon the lion and adder: the young lion and the dragon shalt thou trample under feet.

Psalm 91:10-13

These heavenly hosts have always been present, but the Holy Spirit reveals their presence to us so that we can take advantage of what Jesus has offered us in redemption:

But God hath revealed them unto us by his Spirit: for the Spirit searcheth all things, yea, the deep things of God. For what man knoweth the things of a man, save the spirit of man which is in him? even so the things of God knoweth no man, but the Spirit of God. Now we have received, not the spirit of the world, but the spirit which is of God; that we might know the things that are freely given to us of God. 1 Corinthians 2:10-12

There are heavenly armies that fight for our cause upon the Earth:

> *And one cried unto another, and said, Holy, holy, holy, is the* Lord *of hosts [armies]: the whole earth is full of his glory.* Isaiah 6:3

The moment you declare what God says, these angels go into action. Believe for it, get out of their way, and watch them go into action on your behalf.

The Bible warns us not to let our mouths cause us to sin when it comes to the ministry of angels:

> *Suffer not thy mouth to cause thy flesh to sin; neither say thou before the angel, that it was an error: wherefore should God be angry at thy voice, and destroy the work of thine hands?* Ecclesiastes 5:6

> *Beware of him, and obey his voice, provoke him not; for he will not pardon your transgressions: for my name is in*

> *him. But if thou shalt indeed obey his voice, and do all that I speak; then I will be an enemy unto thine enemies, and an adversary unto thine adversaries.*
>
> Exodus 23:21-22

"My name is in him." Angels act on God's behalf, and His name is in them. The only thing that can possibly stop an angel is something that can stop the name of God, and that doesn't exist.

You are *Destined for Greatness,* but there are things you must understand and put into practice in order to become outstanding.

CHAPTER 6

TAKE THE KEYS AND USE THEM

And to the angel of the church in Philadelphia write; These things saith he that is holy, he that is true, he that hath the key of David, he that openeth, and no man shutteth; and shutteth, and no man openeth. Revelation 3:7

Opening the heavens involves the use of relevant keys. The Word of God shows that I, as an heir of God and joint heir with Christ, have the key of David. This key can open a door that no man can close, and it can close a door that no man can open. What does that mean?

Keys speak of authority, dominion, and power. When you have keys, it's an indication that you are in charge of something. The key of David can be used by anyone of faith, and Jesus said I have that key. Here are some important keys you need to start using:

THE KEY OF COVENANT

Covenant is the bedrock of our confidence in God. Our covenant is a divine agreement between God and man and has an oath based on established terms and principles. God is a covenant-keeping God. This covenant is a surety that God Almighty is committed to us and will stand by His commitments. This was the same key that David used to open doors of victory and triumph.

The Israelites were facing Goliath, and it was like facing an insurmountable mountain. Everything looked like a dead-end. The man was an amazing warrior, and his size was intimidating. He insulted the armies of Israel and called God names, and he did this for forty days without opposition. The people of Israel thought maybe God Himself would respond, and when He didn't, they became very depressed. Then, along came a young man, just a boy really, with a key in his hand that changed everything:

And David spake to the men that stood by him, saying, What shall be done to the man that killeth this Philistine, and taketh away the reproach from Israel? for who is this uncircumcised Philistine, that he should defy the armies of the living God?

Thy servant slew both the lion and the bear: and this uncircumcised Philistine shall be as one of them, seeing he hath defied the armies of the living God.

David said moreover, The LORD that delivered me out of the paw of the lion, and out of the paw of the bear, he will deliver me out of the hand of this Philistine. And Saul said unto David, Go, and the LORD be with thee.

1 Samuel 17:26 and 36-37

David asked, *"Who is this uncircumcised Philistines?"* What did he mean by that? He meant that here was a man with no covenant, and yet he was defying the armies of God? This was not right, and he declared that he would kill this giant of a man.

All that Israel needed was in the camp, but the door had been closed by Goliath's taunts and the fearful responses of God's people. Then, suddenly, David was opening that door simply by invoking the covenant:

> *The enemy shall not exact upon him; nor the son of wickedness afflict him. And I will beat down his foes before his face, and plague them that hate him. But my faithfulness and my mercy shall be with him: and in my name shall his horn be exalted. I will set his hand also in the sea, and his right hand in the rivers.*
> Psalm 89:22-25

David knew that any door could be opened by using the key of covenant:

And I will set up shepherds over them which shall feed them: and they shall fear no more, nor be dismayed, neither shall they be lacking, saith the LORD. Behold, the days come, saith the LORD, that I will raise unto David a righteous Branch, and a King shall reign and prosper, and shall execute judgment and justice in the earth. In his days Judah shall be saved, and Israel shall dwell safely: and this is his name whereby he shall be called, The LORD Our Righteousness

Jeremiah 23:4-6

Once have I sworn by my holiness that I will not lie unto David. His seed shall endure for ever, and his throne as the sun before me. It shall be established for ever as the moon, and as a faithful witness in heaven. Selah.

Psalm 89:35-37

The Messiah came through the lineage of David by covenant. When Jesus walked the Earth, He boldly stated, *"I and my Father are one."* That same covenant is available to you now in and through Christ. Just start using the key of covenant.

Jesus said:

> *And these signs shall follow them that believe; In my name shall they cast out devils; they shall speak with new tongues; they shall take up serpents; and if they drink any deadly thing, it shall not hurt them; they shall lay hands on the sick, and they shall recover.*
>
> Mark 16:17-18

It's a covenant, and it cannot be broken. Use this key and use it wisely.

THE KEY OF THE ANOINTING

The anointing of the Holy Spirit is a divine enablement from God that causes you to do things you could not do in your natural ability. It is the supernatural hand of God upon your life to cause you to excel beyond your natural limits. The anointing will enable you to raise your kids supernaturally, to maintain your health supernaturally, to conduct your business supernaturally, and to manage your home supernaturally.

When the anointing came upon Samson, he was able to kill a lion with his bare hands. When it came upon Jehu, he was able to kill the wicked Queen Jezebel. When it came upon Elijah, he outran the chariot of Ahab. Unusual things happen when the anointing of God comes upon you.

The anointing gives you access to the secrets of God, and it gives you mastery. The anointing was upon Adam before he fell, and he could discern the mind of God and name all the animals God had created. The anointing on Jesus made Him to know all things. That same anointing is upon you now, and you can know things no one else knows.

The Scriptures say:

I have found David my servant; with my holy oil have I anointed him: with whom my hand shall be established: mine arm also shall strengthen him.

> *The enemy shall not exact upon him;*
> *nor the son of wickedness afflict him.*
> *And I will beat down his foes before his*
> *face, and plague them that hate him.*
>   Psalm 89:20-23

It was the anointing that took David to the throne despite every obstacle. Nothing can stop or even hinder the anointing. It is a force that will bring victory to you every time.

Jesus declared:

> *The Spirit of the Lord is upon me, be-*
> *cause he hath anointed me to preach the*
> *gospel to the poor; he hath sent me to*
> *heal the brokenhearted, to preach deliv-*
> *erance to the captives, and recovering of*
> *sight to the blind, to set at liberty them*
> *that are bruised, to preach the acceptable*
> *year of the Lord.*   Luke 4:18-19

This was the key Jesus used, and it changed things everywhere He went. Holy men of old prophesied it:

And it shall come to pass afterward, that I will pour out my spirit upon all flesh; and your sons and your daughters shall prophesy, your old men shall dream dreams, your young men shall see visions: Joel 2:28

So he answered and said to me:

"This is the word of the Lord *to Zerubbabel:*
'Not by might nor by power, but by My Spirit,'
Says the Lord *of hosts.'"*
                      Zechariah 4:6, NKJV

This promised blessing has already been poured out from Heaven. All you need to do is use the key you have been given. When you do, every yoke will be broken, and liberty and breakthrough will come to your life in the name of Jesus Christ.

There are certain things you do in the Kingdom that make so much noise that Heaven cannot rest until your case is resolved. Even when you say nothing, those things speak on your behalf. Situations may not announce their coming, but there is an assurance that there is no way things can prevail against you.

Dorcas died, but Jesus raised her from up from the dead. Peter said of Him:

> *How God anointed Jesus of Nazareth with the Holy Spirit and with power, who went about doing good and healing all who were oppressed by the devil, for God was with Him. And we are witnesses of all things which He did both in the land of the Jews and in Jerusalem, whom they killed by hanging on a tree. Him God raised up on the third day, and showed Him openly, not to all the people, but to witnesses chosen before by God, even to us who ate and drank with Him after He arose from the dead.*
> Acts 10:38-41, NKJV

Many other keys are given to us in the Word of God. Learn them and then use them to open any door. That same anointing has been given to you to bring to life dead things.

You are *Destined for Greatness*, but there are things you must understand and put into practice in order to become outstanding.

CHAPTER 7

DESTINED FOR SUCCESS

Those who come He shall cause to take
root in Jacob;
Israel shall blossom and bud,
And fill the face of the world with fruit.
                                    Isaiah 27:6, NKJV

Success is not just your birthright; it's in your bloodline. The covenant you have with God establishes your success. What God has for you may not be what you expected, but you will be successful because it's in your blood:

> *Let them shout for joy, and be glad,*
> *that favour my righteous cause: yea, let*
> *them say continually, Let the LORD be*

magnified, which hath pleasure in the prosperity of his servant. Psalm 35:27

Yes, God, our Heavenly Father, has *"pleasure in the prosperity of his servant."* And that means you. Moses declared:

> *And the Lord shall make thee the head, and not the tail; and thou shalt be above only, and thou shalt not be beneath; if that thou hearken unto the commandments of the Lord thy God, which I command thee this day, to observe and to do them.* Deuteronomy 28:13

The psalmist declared:

> *Praise ye the Lord. Blessed is the man that feareth the Lord, that delighteth greatly in his commandments. His seed shall be mighty upon earth: the generation of the upright shall be blessed. Wealth and riches shall be in his house: and his righteousness endureth for ever.* Psalm 112:1-3

That is the Almighty speaking to you about His original purpose. But success only comes as we learn God's instructions. He has destined you for trans-generational blessings, but He has also given you guidelines to follow.

Joshua 1:8 shows that prosperity was a function of Old Testament Law:

> *This book of the law shall not depart out of thy mouth; but thou shalt meditate therein day and night, that thou mayest observe to do according to all that is written therein: for then thou shalt make thy way prosperous, and then thou shalt have good success.*

The promises *"thou shalt make thy way prosperous,"* and *"thou shalt have good success,"* are dependant upon the actions outlined in the first part of the verse: *"This book of the law shall not depart out of thy mouth,"* *"thou shalt meditate therein day and night,"* and *"observe to do according to all that is written therein."*

The promised result was to break every barrier and make you a winner in the midst of any and every hardship. That was what happened to Joshua.

If you adhere to the instructions in the book, you will have good success, no matter what. Therefore:

DARE TO BE A DREAMER

The foundation for an enduring success is a dream, and your dream will determine the size of your success. We live in a dreamer's world, and without a dream you're simply out of luck. What you foresee determines where you will go.

God will not dream for you; He will only inspire you. Dreaming is your responsibility. Dream, and dream big!

A man's heart deviseth his way: but the LORD directeth his steps.

Proverbs 16:9

Your dream is the source of your strength. It empowers your faith.

David asked, *"What shall be given to the man who kills this giant and removes the shame from Israel?"* Eternity was already planted on the inside of him, and the same is true of you. Dare to pull it out.

Life looks meaningless without a dream. When there is no dream, confusion reigns. You are packaged with so much from God that impossibilities become possible for you. You are in the class of Elohim. You have been packaged to birth greatness.

We all start with doubts, like "Who am I among so many people?" But that's because we don't yet know the greatness of what has been invested in us. Saul, before he became king, had these same doubts. Samuel addressed them:

> *And as for thine asses that were lost three days ago, set not thy mind on them; for they are found. And on whom is all the desire of Israel? Is it not on thee, and on all thy father's house? And*

Saul answered and said, Am not I a Benjamite, of the smallest of the tribes of Israel? and my family the least of all the families of the tribe of Benjamin? wherefore then speakest thou so to me?
1 Samuel 9:20-21

The desire of the entire nation was on Saul, and yet he somehow couldn't see that fact. Never forget that like begets like, and every fruit carries the seed of the parent. If you come from God, there is a God on the inside of you:

Now unto him that is able to do exceeding abundantly above all that we ask or think, according to the power that worketh in us. Ephesians 3:20

BE SPECIFIC ABOUT WHAT YOU WANT IN LIFE

Your Father owns this estate called Earth, and you are a joint heir with Jesus Christ. You were not intended to be managed; you were destined to be the manager. There is nothing that shapes destiny and brings inner glory more quickly than being specific about what you want in life.

The world around us is full of distractions. If you don't know what you want, it will affect where you are going. The good news is that no matter what you want to become in life, it is already packaged in you by God. *"All things that pertain to life and godliness"* are in you:

> *According as his divine power hath given unto us all things that pertain unto life and godliness, through the knowledge of him that hath called us to glory and virtue.* 2 Peter 1:3

All that is needed is your total dependence on God and your self-discipline. That is what it will take to achieve your dream. There is no limit to your rising, no cap whatsoever. Jesus has already said that you were to do *"greater works"* even than He did here:

Verily, verily, I say unto you, He that believeth on me, the works that I do shall he do also; and greater works than these shall he do; because I go unto my Father. John 14:12

What people say or what you feel have nothing to do with your dream. You are God's dream come true, and His wish for you is blessing. He said:

For I know the thoughts that I think toward you, saith the LORD, thoughts of peace, and not of evil, to give you an expected end. Jeremiah 29:11

Change your thought to match God's thoughts, and you will see a greater tomorrow. God sees you as being *"on high above all"*:

And it shall come to pass, if thou shalt hearken diligently unto the voice of the LORD thy God, to observe and to do all his commandments which I command thee this day, that the LORD thy God will set thee on high above all nations of the earth: and all these blessings shall come on thee, and overtake thee, if thou shalt hearken unto the voice of the LORD *thy God.* Deuteronomy 28:1-2

It is not the devil who kills a lot of your dreams; it is you allowing the dream God planted in you to lie dormant. If you fail to sharpen your dream and keep it alive, it will surely die, or, as so often happens, lose its fervor. Stop procrastinating and start winning.

If your dream is real, the devil will fight it, but the fact that there is opposition is proof that the dream is indeed real. Every seed fights to break out of the ground, and you must fight to see your dream realized.

Nobody has a right to demean your mission, for they didn't send you. No man or woman has the right to minimize your dream, for they didn't give it to you. Be responsible enough to believe God, and then do whatever you have to do to get yourself to your eternal destination in Him.

DISCOVER YOUR POTENTIAL AND STICK WITH IT

There is a level of potential in you that God put there, and it is enough to make you a star and to give you an edge among other humans. The same grace and power that was in Christ is now in you. In fact, the Bible says very clearly that you have the mind of Christ:

> *For who hath known the mind of the Lord, that he may instruct him? but we have the mind of Christ.*
>
> 1 Corinthians 2:16

None of us is empty or useless. We have all been loaded. The difference is in our level of discovery. Fish came out of water, so a fish is water. Animals came out of dirt, so an animal is one hundred percent dirt. We, however, came out of God, so man is God-like.

Don't be deceived by your exterior, your house, your body. Inside it is the image and likeness of God Almighty Himself.

We live in an unfinished world, and what God put inside of you was with the intent that you would finish the unfinished world. Therefore, challenge yourself, your gifts, and your desires. Do something different, something unique.

The reason you are restless is because the glory of God in you wants to manifest, and it's time. It can wait no more. Why not give it a try now? Start the school, the business, or whatever else God has put in your heart. You can do it:

> *I can do all things through Christ which strengtheneth me.* Philippians 4:13

Yes, you, too, can do *"all things."*

GET RID OF COMPLAINING OR MURMURING

No matter what, God's got you, so stop complaining or murmuring. If you are experiencing a wilderness, that's an indication that you are approaching your Promised

Land. Your wilderness experience is merely a time of training and character development. Instead of complaining, open yourself up for the necessary learning. If you are bitter and frustrated, you can't learn anything.

Things may not seem to be going your way right now, but they will come around. God does not fail, and if you follow His plan, you will get there—no matter what the enemy does.

The devil cannot stop you, so stay encouraged. God will never abandon you. Remain open to Him and ask Him what you should do and how you should do it. The devil wants you to quit. Don't give in to him. Never faint:

> *Therefore seeing we have this ministry, as we have received mercy, we faint not.* 2 Corinthians 4:1

When you know that your destiny is custom-made by Heaven, you can laugh at every situation. God is working in you, and whatever the Lord does is for eternity:

I will go before thee, and make the crooked places straight: I will break in pieces the gates of brass, and cut in sunder the bars of iron. Isaiah 45:2

Make a holy declaration today:

Father, in the name of Jesus Christ, I command every limitation to be removed in my life right now in Jesus' name. You promised:

> *For thou shalt break forth on the right hand and on the left; and thy seed shall inherit the Gentiles, and make the desolate cities to be inhabited.* Isaiah 54:3

Father, in the name of Jesus Christ, I am breaking forth now in every area of my life. I am taking my rightful place in Jesus' name. You said:

> *But my God shall supply all your need according to his riches in glory by Christ Jesus.* Philippians 4:19

Father, in the name of Jesus Christ, everything needed for my outstanding results is being released to me right now in Jesus' name. Your Word declares:

> *For if by the one man's offense death reigned through the one, much more those who receive abundance of grace and of the gift of righteousness will reign in life through the One, Jesus Christ.* Romans 5:17, NKJV

Redemption forbids your failure. Failure for a child of God? Never!

> *Giving thanks unto the Father, which hath made us meet to be partakers of the inheritance of the saints in light: who hath delivered us from the power of darkness, and hath translated us into the kingdom of his dear Son.*
> Colossians 1:12-13

We have an inheritance because we left the kingdom of lack and have been translated into the Kingdom of light. Our mandate is to break forth until we take over:

> *For thou shalt break forth on the right hand and on the left; and thy seed shall inherit the Gentiles, and make the desolate cities to be inhabited.* Isaiah 54:3

You are breaking forth now in the name of Jesus Christ. No more barriers henceforth in Jesus' name! God has spoken, and nothing can stop it.

Your journey started with God and not with your parents. It was for the process of bringing you here that your parents were involved. They were used by God to bring His dream to the Earth. You didn't come here of your own will. It was not because you prayed. God Himself brought you here as His dream come true. Therefore, it was not an option for you. Realizing this, David sang:

> *I will praise thee; for I am fearfully and wonderfully made: marvellous are thy*

> *works; and that my soul knoweth right*
> *well.*   Psalm 139:14

You, too, are *"fearfully and wonderfully made,"* signifying that you are a born success and are here for a purpose. You are here on assignment, sent by God, and because of that, no man or woman and no devil can stop you from achieving your fullness except you.

Just as the sun cannot be stopped from shining in the day, neither the moon resisted from shining in the night, nothing can stop you from reigning now in Jesus' name. It is only when you walk contrary to the covenant that you lose your bearings. Whether a saint or an unbeliever, everyone wants to succeed. How sad that the enemy has deceived so many into following him, for what he has promised them will not last:

> *Again, the devil taketh him up into an*
> *exceeding high mountain, and sheweth*
> *him all the kingdoms of the world, and*

the glory of them; and saith unto him, All these things will I give thee, if thou wilt fall down and worship me.
Matthew 4:8-9

Just as the evil one told Jesus, "Bow down to me, and I will give you the world and its glory," you must know what is written about you so you won't bow to his manipulations and what step or steps to take to win. The winning gene is in you:

Which were born, not of blood, nor of the will of the flesh, nor of the will of man, but of God.   John 1:13

You are *Destined for Greatness,* but there are things you must understand and put into practice in order to become outstanding.

CHAPTER 8

"BY HIS SPIRIT THAT DWELLETH IN YOU"

But if the Spirit of him that raised up Jesus from the dead dwell in you, he that raised up Christ from the dead shall also quicken your mortal bodies by his Spirit that dwelleth in you. Romans 8:11

UNDERSTAND THAT YOU ARE A SPIRIT, AN EXPRESSION OF ETERNITY, AND LEARN TO LISTEN TO THE INNER WITNESS

Inside of you is the same Spirit that raised Jesus from the dead. You are more than what can be seen from the outside, and you are stronger than what the people around you think, for your root is in God through Christ, and that puts you in a class with divinity:

Herein is our love made perfect, that we may have boldness in the day of judgment: because as he is, so are we in this world. 1 John 4:17

Therefore, you must do what Jesus did when He was on the Earth. He said:

I can of mine own self do nothing: as I hear, I judge: and my judgment is just; because I seek not mine own will, but the will of the Father which hath sent me. John 5:30

We all want success in life, but not many other people really want you to succeed. They don't see what you see and what God put in your heart. Listen to God, and men will adjust to your dream.

If the people around you despise your dream and you agree with them, you have denied the power that put that dream in your heart in the first place. To be delivered from the devil is often much easier than being delivered from people. That takes effort on your part:

> *But rise, and stand upon thy feet: for I have appeared unto thee for this purpose, to make thee a minister and a witness both of these things which thou hast seen, and of those things in the which I will appear unto thee; delivering thee from the people, and from the Gentiles, unto whom now I send thee.* Acts 26:16-17

Not everyone will believe what God shows and tells you. The believing must start with you. Refuse to let go of your dream. If God has spoken, stick to what He has said without wavering. If He said it, then you have it already. If all you want is the approval of men, you will miss what God has for you. There is a voice inside of you speaking. Don't despise it. That voice is your solution:

For as many as are led by the Spirit of God, they are the sons of God.
The Spirit itself beareth witness with our spirit, that we are the children of God. Romans 8:14 and 16

INCREASE YOUR CAPACITY AND KNOW YOUR CAPABILITIES

God never puts a cap or a limit on you, so don't put one on yourself. He said that you can do all things through Christ. so don't be satisfied to build a hamlet when you could build a city.

You are limitless, but the future is dependent upon you and your readiness to explore. You don't need anybody's permission to enlarge yourself. All it takes is your willingness to seek the answers to life's question. The quality of your questions will be determined by the level of your thirst. Ask the right questions, and be determined to get answers.

This search for answers will increase your capacity. If your container holds only five liters, you cannot put twenty liters of water in it. The questions you ask create a thirst and end in a search and an enlargement of your capacity

The world is full of questions and problems. The problem you learn to solve creates a job for you, instead of you looking for a job, and men will seek you out.

ADD VALUE TO YOURSELF

People won't pay you for what you're worth but for the value you have added to yourself. If you add value to yourself, the world will gladly pay for it. It is not just discovering your gifts that matters; refining and putting to practical use those gifts is what really counts. The world is always looking for solutions. If you provide them, the world will come knocking on your door.

So many choose to live "a normal life" when just adding a little to themselves could make them outstanding among men. Your responsibility brings unlimited possibilities.

Use Your Faith

Beloved, don't just have faith in God; use your faith in God. Put it to work. Faith gives you ownership. It puts you in control.

Faith sees what your eyes cannot see. It gives you access to your divine right, and this, in turn, gives you authority over every demonic power. Faith will pull you out of every pit:

> *Simon Peter, a servant and an apostle of Jesus Christ, to them that have obtained like precious faith with us through the righteousness of God and our Saviour Jesus Christ: Grace and peace be multiplied unto you through the knowledge of God, and of Jesus our Lord, according as his divine power hath given unto us all things that pertain unto life and godliness, through the knowledge of him that hath called us to glory and virtue: whereby are given unto us exceeding great and precious promises: that by these ye might be partakers of the divine*

nature, having escaped the corruption that is in the world through lust. And beside this, giving all diligence, add to your faith virtue; and to virtue knowl-edge.   2 Peter 1:1-5

Faith takes you to a place where you can-not be controlled by any situation. You can now live as if you own it because you do.

Faith manifests in miracles, and faith gives you ownership:

And he said unto her, Daughter, thy faith hath made thee whole; go in peace, and be whole of thy plague.

As soon as Jesus heard the word that was spoken, he saith unto the ruler of the synagogue, Be not afraid, only believe. And he suffered no man to follow him, save Peter, and James, and John the brother of James. And he cometh to the house of the ruler of the synagogue, and seeth the tumult, and them that wept and wailed greatly.
                          Mark 5:34 and 36-38

You own a thing the minute you believe it. The greatest faith is to see Jesus in every situation. Every impossibility becomes possible when you believe and receive all that God says is true about you.

If you only believe what you see and feel, you will have an aborted faith. We are to live and believe what God says, not what we see, and He has said that Christ dwells in us now. Period!

Redemption confers on you all the ability of Heaven to do exploits. Therefore, you have everything it takes to be more than a conqueror. Yes, you have authority over demons, powers of darkness, and evil, even over death.

My assignment from God is to teach men wisdom and understanding. If you will obey these revelations, wisdom and understanding will bring you to an unusual multiplication and to greatness:

And I will give you pastors according to mine heart, which shall feed you with knowledge and understanding.

*And it shall come to pass, when ye be multiplied and increased in the land, in those days, saith the L*ORD*, they shall say no more, The ark of the covenant of the L*ORD*: neither shall it come to mind: neither shall they remember it; neither shall they visit it; neither shall that be done any more.*   Jeremiah 3:15-16

When life is void of the supernatural, oppression and bondage quickly settle in. Actually, nothing submits to you in life unless you overpower it. Without power, life is uncomfortable. I hear God speaking to us today as He did in the beginning:

And God said, Let us make man in our image, after our likeness: and let them have dominion over the fish of the sea, and over the fowl of the air, and over the cattle, and over all the earth, and over every creeping thing that creepeth upon the earth.
And God blessed them, and God said unto them, Be fruitful, and multiply, and replenish the earth, and subdue it:

> *and have dominion over the fish of the*
> *sea, and over the fowl of the air, and over*
> *every living thing that moveth upon the*
> *earth.*   Genesis 1:26 and 28

Here is proof that you cannot be in charge without power:

> *Say unto God, How terrible art thou*
> *in thy works! through the greatness of*
> *thy power shall thine enemies submit*
> *themselves unto thee.*   Psalm 66:3

Even Jesus could not do mighty works here until heavenly power came to Him. Without that heavenly touch, He would have been devoid of exploits:

> *How God anointed Jesus of Nazareth*
> *with the Holy Ghost and with power:*
> *who went about doing good, and healing*
> *all that were oppressed of the devil; for*
> *God was with him.*   Acts 10:38

Doing good is beyond our natural power. Jesus was the *"beloved Son of God"*:

> *Now when all the people were baptized, it came to pass, that Jesus also being baptized, and praying, the heaven was opened, and the Holy Ghost descended in a bodily shape like a dove upon him, and a voice came from heaven, which said, Thou art my beloved Son; in thee I am well pleased.* Luke 3:21-22

Still, He did miracles only after the power came to Him:

> *And Jesus returned in the power of the Spirit into Galilee: and there went out a fame of him through all the region round about.* Luke 4:14

Exploits begin with power, not with mouthing religion platitudes. Jesus warned His disciples that without power they would be mocked. Therefore, He commanded them, *"Tarry in Jerusalem*

173

until you are endued with power from on high":

> *And, behold, I send the promise of my Father upon you: but tarry ye in the city of Jerusalem, until ye be endued with power from on high.* Luke 24:49

The disciples obeyed, and the promise of Acts 1:8 came about:

> *But ye shall receive power, after that the Holy Ghost is come upon you: and ye shall be witnesses unto me both in Jerusalem, and in all Judaea, and in Samaria, and unto the uttermost part of the earth.*

Your success is proof of God's faithfulness and love:

> *Even every one that is called by my name: for I have created him for my glory, I have formed him; yea, I have made him.* Isaiah 43:7

There is a dimension of the manifestation of the Spirit of God that makes things happen in our lives, and it is totally beyond human understanding.

We all came here as giants to experience life, but Satan wants to make dwarfs of us. God has made provision to raise you up from nothing and put you in charge. You may feel scattered, dry, and hopeless, but God is pouring out His Spirit on you, and the warrior in you will rise today in Jesus' name.

In Joel's time, God promised to pour out His Spirit in the last days:

> *And it shall come to pass afterward, that I will pour out my spirit upon all flesh; and your sons and your daughters shall prophesy, your old men shall dream dreams, your young men shall see visions.* Joel 2:28

The Spirit of God is what it takes to make a champion of any one, no matter their condition. Bezalleel was a name no one recognized until the touch of God came upon him:

And the LORD spake unto Moses, saying, See, I have called by name Bezaleel the son of Uri, the son of Hur, of the tribe of Judah: and I have filled him with the spirit of God, in wisdom, and in understanding, and in knowledge, and in all manner of workmanship.

Exodus 31:1-3

Your story is also changing, and it can happen right now. Why? Because God is no respecter of persons:

Then Peter opened his mouth, and said, Of a truth I perceive that God is no respecter of persons: but in every nation he that feareth him, and worketh righteousness, is accepted with him.

Acts 10:34-35

You are *Destined for Greatness,* but there are things you must understand and put into practice in order to become outstanding.

CHAPTER 9

YOUR SITUATION IS NOT A PROBLEM FOR GOD

When thou passest through the waters, I will be with thee; and through the rivers, they shall not overflow thee: when thou walkest through the fire, thou shalt not be burned; neither shall the flame kindle upon thee.   Isaiah 43:2

We have all read about the manifestation of God's power and glory in the valley of dry bones in Ezekiel 37, and the awesome fact is that God has not changed. He knows your present situation and is not confused or embarrassed about bailing you out. What Ezekiel saw before him was devastating:

> *And caused me to pass by them round*
> *about: and, behold, there were very*
> *many in the open valley; and, lo, they*
> *were very dry.*   Ezekiel 37:2

There is no situation that confronts you in which God is lacking a solution. The secret is you can't concentrate on the problem; you have to concentrate on God, for He is the Solution. As you do this, your situation will change.

All too often we limit God by not speaking what we are commanded to say in a given situation. The Spirit is just waiting for your declaration. Then, He will go into action:

> *Say unto them, As truly as I live, saith*
> *the Lord, as ye have spoken in mine ears,*
> *so will I do to you.*   Numbers 14:28

> *His mother saith unto the servants,*
> *Whatsoever he saith unto you, do it.*
>   John 2:5

God is not confused; He just doesn't see things the way we see them. With Him, there are no impossibilities. Whatever He says, that's the answer:

Again he said unto me, Prophesy upon these bones, and say unto them, O ye dry bones, hear the word of the LORD. Thus saith the LORD God unto these bones; Behold, I will cause breath to enter into you, and ye shall live: and I will lay sinews upon you, and will bring up flesh upon you, and cover you with skin, and put breath in you, and ye shall live; and ye shall know that I am the LORD. So I prophesied as I was commanded: and as I prophesied, there was a noise, and behold a shaking, and the bones came together, bone to his bone. Ezekiel 37:4-7

Your present situation does not and cannot stop God from working. Those bones were *"very dry,"* but God knew that, and it didn't bother Him:

Then said he unto me, Prophesy unto the wind, prophesy, son of man, and say to the wind, Thus saith the LORD God; Come from the four winds, O breath, and breathe upon these slain, that they may live. So I prophesied as he commanded me, and the breath came into them, and they lived, and stood up upon their feet, an exceeding great army.

Ezekiel 37:9-10

Believe that whatever has been scattered can be gathered:

So I prophesied as I was commanded: and as I prophesied, there was a noise, and behold a shaking, and the bones came together, bone to his bone.

Ezekiel 37:7

To give up in any situation is to insult God, to limit the Holy One of Israel. What men have told you or what seems to be the situation before you is really a mirage. The truth is that God is putting you over others, and what you are now experiencing is nothing more than a test of your faith. God said:

Behold, I am the LORD, the God of all flesh: is there any thing too hard for me?   Jeremiah 32:27

As you view your current situation, know that the Holy Spirit can create something from nothing. He proved that in the beginning:

In the beginning God created the heaven and the earth. And the earth was without form, and void; and darkness was upon the face of the deep. And the Spirit of God moved upon the face of the waters. And God said, Let there be light: and there was light.   Genesis 1:1-3

Thou sendest forth thy spirit, they are created: and thou renewest the face of the earth.   Psalm 104:30

Every dry situation in your life is being revived today in the name of Jesus. Know that the Spirit of God can even open graves and cause the dead to rise:

Therefore prophesy and say unto them, Thus saith the LORD God; Behold, O my people, I will open your graves, and cause you to come up out of your graves, and bring you into the land of Israel. And ye shall know that I am the LORD, when I have opened your graves, O my people, and brought you up out of your graves, and shall put my spirit in you, and ye shall live, and I shall place you in your own land: then shall ye know that I the LORD have spoken it, and performed it, saith the LORD.

Ezekiel 37:12-14

When God is involved, there is nothing terminal, and there are no closed doors—never. A grave speaks of dead cases, irreversible situations, closed cases. But God says, *"I will open your graves."* What more could we ask for?

The wind of God's Spirit is blowing over you right now, and whatever is dead or dry is coming back to life. His Word declares:

For the invisible things of him from the creation of the world are clearly seen, being understood by the things that are made, even his eternal power and Godhead; so that they are without excuse. Romans 1:20

The invisible become to visible so that you might understand the language of the Spirit. It happened in Samuel's time:

Then Samuel took the horn of oil, and anointed him [David] in the midst of his brethren: and the Spirit of the LORD came upon David from that day forward. So Samuel rose up, and went to Ramah. 1 Samuel 16:13

What happened that changed everything that day?

It shall come to pass in that day That his burden will be taken away from your shoulder, And his yoke from your neck, And the yoke will be

183

> *destroyed because of the anointing oil.* Isaiah 10:27, NKJV

> *Then he said to me, "This [continuous supply of oil] is the word of the LORD to Zerubbabel [prince of Judah], saying, 'Not by might, nor by power, but by My Spirit [of whom the oil is a symbol],' says the LORD of hosts."* Zechariah 4:6, AMP

This anointing of power came upon David, and it's coming upon you too, right now in Jesus' name.

God is saying to us all: "Believe Me and believe the prophets I send to you":

> *So they got up early in the morning and went out into the Wilderness of Tekoa; and as they went out, Jehoshaphat stood and said, "Hear me, O Judah, and you inhabitants of Jerusalem! Believe and trust in the LORD your God and you will be established (secure). Believe and trust in His prophets and succeed."*
> 2 Chronicles 20:20, AMP

With this anointing oil upon your life, you will escape every delay on your way to greatness. Those obstacles are removed. According to the Word of the Lord, every abandoned project in your life is to be completed in Jesus' name. Every venom of the wicked is paralyzed today in the name of Jesus.

At one point, the Israelites were dying in the wilderness by the thousands because of snake bites. That poison was causing horrible complications. But God told Moses to make a serpent of brass and hang it on a tree, and whoever looked up to it would escape death. Moses obeyed, and those who looked lived. Those who doubted the simplicity of this solution died (see Numbers 21). Of this, Jesus preached:

> *No one has ascended to heaven but He who came down from heaven, that is, the Son of Man who is in heaven. And as Moses lifted up the serpent in the wilderness, even so must the Son of Man be lifted up, that whoever believes in Him should not perish but have eternal life.*
>
> John 3:13-15, NKJV

Every poison of the serpent, the devil and his cohorts is paralyzed and destroyed now. The serpent still bites, but Jesus is here to save us.

God anointed Jesus to destroy the works of the devil. His work was vividly described by John:

> *The thief cometh not, but for to steal, and to kill, and to destroy: I am come that they might have life, and that they might have it more abundantly.*
>
> John 10:10

Beloved, if you know the love of God for you, you will ignore the devil and his taunts and take authority over every sickness and every disease:

> *And when he had called unto him his twelve disciples, he gave them power against unclean spirits, to cast them out, and to heal all manner of sickness and all manner of disease.*
>
> Matthew 10:1

"All manner" ... that's what God's Word says. Because I am one of those sent by Jesus Christ, I place judgment upon sickness and disease, lack and oppression, and I destroy their hold on God's people now in Jesus' name.

A major part of Jesus' ministry on the Earth was to heal the sick. He is *"the Saviour of the body"*:

> *For the husband is the head of the wife,*
> *even as Christ is the head of the church:*
> *and he is the saviour of the body.*
> Ephesians 5:23

He heals our bodies because they become His home:

> *But Christ as a son over his own house;*
> *whose house are we, if we hold fast the*
> *confidence and the rejoicing of the hope*
> *firm unto the end.* Hebrews 3:6

Jesus told His disciples to preach the Gospel and heal the sick:

*And he sent them to preach the kingdom
of God, and to heal the sick.* Luke 9:2

When the disciples came back, they said,
*"Even the devils are subject unto us through
thy name":*

*And the seventy returned again with joy,
saying, Lord, even the devils are subject
unto us through thy name.* Luke 10:17

Jesus answered them:

*And he said unto them, I beheld Satan
as lightning fall from heaven.*
Luke 10:18

He is fallen and defeated. Therefore, wher-
ever you are operating for the sake of Jesus
Christ and in His name, you can tell devils,
"Get out, and get out now!"
Jesus boldly proclaimed:

*Therefore let all the house of Israel know
assuredly, that God hath made the same*

Jesus, whom ye have crucified, both Lord and Christ. Acts 2:36

The Lord is there with you now. Tell the demons to get out in His name, just as Jesus did:

And Jesus went about all Galilee, teaching in their synagogues, and preaching the gospel of the Kingdom, and healing all manner of sickness and all manner of disease among the people. And his fame went throughout all Syria: and they brought unto him all sick people that were taken with divers diseases and torments, and those which were possessed with devils, and those which were lunatick, and those that had the palsy; and he healed them.
Matthew 4:23-24

Because Jesus was preaching the Gospel of the Kingdom, this represented an invasion, a change of government, Heaven taking over the affairs of the Earth. In the process, He ran out

the oppressors, and they were forced to flee.
You don't have to be sick and oppressed or die
young and poor. Kingdom preaching declares
that your sins are completely forgiven, as if
they never existed in the first place. So, come
back home. Father is waiting for you with open
arms.

Jesus came here on a mission, and He
fulfilled it. His mission was to destroy the
works of the devil. The Bible states that He
"fulfilled all that was written of him":

> *And when they had fulfilled all that was
> written of him, they took him down from
> the tree, and laid him in a sepulchre.*
> Acts 13:29

Your sickness and disease were part of
what Jesus fulfilled that day, and the commission He gave when He rose from the
dead was for us to now cast out devils and
heal the sick in His name:

> *And these signs shall follow them that
> believe; In my name shall they cast*

*out devils; they shall speak with new
tongues.*   Mark 16:17

Sickness is from the devil, never from
God. Job was deceived and thought his
affliction was God dealing with him and
teaching him something. He said, "S*hall
we receive good at the hand of God, and shall
we not receive evil?"*

> *But he said unto her [his wife], Thou
> speakest as one of the foolish women
> speaketh. What? shall we receive good at
> the hand of God, and shall we not receive
> evil? In all this did not Job sin with his
> lips.*   Job 2:10

But Job's suffering was definitely not from
God. The Bible makes it very clear that it
was Satan who smote him:

> *So went Satan forth from the presence
> of the* LORD, *and smote Job with sore
> boils from the sole of his foot unto his
> crown.*   Job 2:7

Only good gifts come from God, for He is the Father of Light, not of darkness. Sickness and disease are a curse, not a blessing—never:

> *But it shall come to pass, if thou wilt not hearken unto the voice of the LORD thy God, to observe to do all his commandments and his statutes which I command thee this day; that all these curses shall come upon thee, and overtake thee.*
>
> *Then the LORD will make thy plagues wonderful, and the plagues of thy seed, even great plagues, and of long continuance, and sore sicknesses, and of long continuance. Moreover he will bring upon thee all the diseases of Egypt, which thou wast afraid of; and they shall cleave unto thee. Also every sickness, and every plague, which is not written in the book of this law, them will the LORD bring upon thee, until thou be destroyed.*
>
> Deuteronomy 28:15 and 59-61

God had told Abraham that He would curse those who cursed him and bless those who blessed him:

> *And I will bless them that bless thee, and curse him that curseth thee: and in thee shall all families of the earth be blessed.*   Genesis 12:3

Galatians 3:29 shows us that we are now *"heirs according to the promise"*:

> *And if ye be Christ's, then are ye Abraham's seed, and heirs according to the promise.*

Galatians 3:13-14 agrees:

> *Christ hath redeemed us from the curse of the law, being made a curse for us: for it is written, Cursed is every one that hangeth on a tree: that the blessing of Abraham might come on the Gentiles through Jesus Christ; that we might receive the promise of the Spirit through faith.*

You are *Destined for Greatness*, but there are things you must understand and put into practice in order to become outstanding.

CHAPTER 10

DESTINED FOR GREATNESS

The LORD our God spake unto us in Horeb, saying, Ye have dwelt long enough in this mount: turn you, and take your journey, and go to the mount of the Amorites, and unto all the places nigh thereunto, in the plain, in the hills, and in the vale, and in the south, and by the sea side, to the land of the Canaanites, and unto Lebanon, unto the great river, the river Euphrates.

Deuteronomy 1:6-7

It's time for the next level, and that level comes with the application of Kingdom principles. That is what will cause us to excel here on Earth. To be stagnant and limited is contrary to our covenant with God. He has called us to advance.

God has made provision in His Word, showing us how to ascend to a new level, and by using His wisdom we can reach our maximum accomplishments. It's amazing to think, but the Scriptures clearly say that our Heavenly Father knows exactly what we need and has made provision for it. All He requires of us is that we *"seek"* Him first:

> *But first and most importantly seek (aim at, strive after) His kingdom and His righteousness [His way of doing and being right — the attitude and character of God], and all these things will be given to you also.*
>
> Matthew 6:33, AMP

When nothing seems to be happening, life is naturally boring and frustrating, and that is not God's will for us. There is a way of doing things in the Kingdom. It's not psychology or philosophy, not even science. It is adhering to the dictates of the King Himself.

Sweating and toiling in order to rise in life is contrary to our God-given covenant. Jesus said, *"My yoke is easy and my burden is light"* (KJV):

> *Come to Me, all who are weary and heavily burdened [by religious rituals that provide no peace], and I will give you rest [refreshing your souls with salvation]. Take My yoke upon you and learn from Me [following Me as My disciple], for I am gentle and humble in heart, and you will find rest (renewal, blessed quiet) for your souls.*
>
> Matthew 11:28-29, AMP

There is a way to rise that the world is not aware of. Kingdom citizens are empowered by God to excel where others have struggled. This mandate does not come from man, but from God. Never forget that. Moses prophesied:

> *The LORD will open for you His good treasure house, the heavens, to give rain*

to your land in its season and to bless all
the work of your hand; and you will lend
to many nations, but you will not bor-
row. The LORD *will make you the head*
(leader) and not the tail (follower); and
you will be above only, and you will not
be beneath, if you listen and pay atten-
tion to the commandments of the LORD
your God, which I am commanding you
today, to observe them carefully.
Deuteronomy 28:12-13, AMP

The next level for you is a function of your mindset based on God's truth. He will never place barriers on your path, so no matter what you see as a stumbling block, it cannot prevail against you or stop you. You are a barrier-breaker, and God has already filled you with power and glory to rule the Universe. The psalmist proclaimed:

For by thee I have run through a troop;
and by my God have I leaped over a
wall. Psalm 18:29

The enemy's desire is to put you in a box through the people and situations around you. Refuse to be boxed in. Your environment must not dictate your destiny. You determine for yourself what your environment will be:

> *And God blessed them, and God said unto them, Be fruitful, and multiply, and replenish the earth, and subdue it: and have dominion over the fish of the sea, and over the fowl of the air, and over every living thing that moveth upon the earth.*   Genesis 1:28

Understand the Extensive Power of the Covenant

In this perverse world full of deceit and wickedness, it takes an understanding of our covenant with God to excel. The Bible says that although we are *"of God,"* the *"whole world lies in wickedness"*:

And we know that we are of God, and the whole world lieth in wickedness.

1 John 5:19

It is covenant blessings that will cause you to rise while others are sinking:

Have respect unto the covenant: for the dark places of the earth are full of the habitations of cruelty.   Psalm 74:20

God is a God of covenant, and He keeps His covenants. Our covenant is an agreement between God and man ratified with an oath based on Jesus' blood. It is the foundation to an unwavering faith and confidence because the oath of God is involved, and God is not an oath-breaker. While it does not make sense to man, the covenant of God goes into action. It came with a vow from God:

For when God made promise to Abraham, because he could swear by no greater, he sware by himself, saying, Surely bless-ing I will bless thee, and multiplying

200

*I will multiply thee. And so, after he
had patiently endured, he obtained the
promise.*

*For men verily swear by the greater:
and an oath for confirmation is to them
an end of all strife. Wherein God, willing more abundantly to shew unto the
heirs of promise the immutability of his
counsel, confirmed it by an oath: that
by two immutable things, in which it
was impossible for God to lie, we might
have a strong consolation, who have fled
for refuge to lay hold upon the hope set
before us: which hope we have as an an-
chor of the soul, both sure and stedfast,
and which entereth into that within the
veil.* Hebrews 6:13-19

God gave His word, and that was the
end of the discussion. That was why, when
Abraham was tested, he did not consider the
age or condition of his body or that of Sarah.
The covenant was involved, so that settled it.
God had promised, and God would deliver
on His promise:

And also that nation, whom they shall serve, will I judge: and afterward shall they come out with great substance. And thou shalt go to thy fathers in peace; thou shalt be buried in a good old age.   Genesis 15:14-15

As for me, behold, my covenant is with thee, and thou shalt be a father of many nations. Neither shall thy name any more be called Abram, but thy name shall be Abraham; for a father of many nations have I made thee. And I will make thee exceeding fruitful, and I will make nations of thee, and kings shall come out of thee. And I will establish my covenant between me and thee and thy seed after thee in their generations for an everlasting covenant, to be a God unto thee, and to thy seed after thee.   Genesis 17:4-7

And I will bless them that bless thee, and curse him that curseth thee: and in thee shall all families of the earth be blessed.   Genesis 12:3

This covenant is still valid in New Testament times:

And if ye be Christ's, then are ye Abraham's seed, and heirs according to the promise. Galatians 3:29

When the people of Israel were in bondage in Egypt, they cried out, and God remembered His covenant and delivered them:

And it came to pass in process of time, that the king of Egypt died: and the children of Israel sighed by reason of the bondage, and they cried, and their cry came up unto God by reason of the bondage. And God heard their groaning, and God remembered his covenant with Abraham, with Isaac, and with Jacob. And God looked upon the children of Israel, and God had respect unto them. Exodus 2:23-25

You, too, have been delivered. Let your deliverance manifest right now.

I am in a covenant with the God of Heaven and Earth, and that is the key to the next level. I cannot fail, and the same is true for you.

The covenant of God is expressed in words. The Bible calls it *"the words of this covenant"*:

> *Keep therefore the words of this covenant, and do them, that ye may prosper in all that ye do.*   Deuteronomy 29:9

> *My covenant will I not break, nor alter the thing that is gone out of my lips. Once have I sworn by my holiness that I will not lie unto David.*
> Psalm 89:34-35

God declared that the strength of the covenant is as long as the sun shines in the day and moon by night:

> *Thus saith the LORD; If ye can break my covenant of the day, and my covenant of the night, and that there should not be*

day and night in their season; then may also my covenant be broken with David my servant, that he should not have a son to reign upon his throne; and with the Levites the priests, my ministers. Thus saith the LORD; If my covenant be not with day and night, and if I have not appointed the ordinances of heaven and earth; then will I cast away the seed of Jacob and David my servant, so that I will not take any of his seed to be rulers over the seed of Abraham, Isaac, and Jacob: for I will cause their captivity to return, and have mercy on them.

Jeremiah 33:20-21 and 25-26

That settles it. So, look into the covenant and then invoke it by faith in the name of Jesus Christ:

The LORD shall open unto thee his good treasure, the heaven to give the rain unto thy land in his season, and to bless all the work of thine hand: and thou shalt lend unto many nations, and thou shalt not borrow. And the Lord shall make thee the head, and not the tail; and thou shalt be above only, and thou shalt not be beneath; if that thou hearken unto the commandments of the Lord thy God, which I command thee this day, to observe and to do them.

Deuteronomy 28:12-13

Believe for the Favor of God upon Your Life

Your next level is a function of God's favor upon you based upon His covenant. We can see this in the life of Joseph:

And Joseph was brought down to Egypt; and Potiphar, an officer of Pharaoh, captain of the guard, an Egyptian, bought him of the hands of the Ishmeelites, which had brought him down thither.
And the Lord was with Joseph, and he was a prosperous man; and he was in the house of his master the Egyptian.

And his master saw that the LORD *was with him, and that the* LORD *made all that he did to prosper in his hand.*

And Joseph found grace in his sight, and he served him: and he made him overseer over his house, and all that he had he put into his hand. And it came to pass from the time that he had made him overseer in his house, and over all that he had, that the LORD *blessed the Egyptian's house for Joseph's sake; and the blessing of the* LORD *was upon all that he had in the house, and in the field. And he left all that he had in Joseph's hand; and he knew not ought he had, save the bread which he did eat. And Joseph was a goodly person, and well favoured.* Genesis 39:1-6

God was with Joseph, and so he prospered everywhere he went, and the glory of God upon His life opened doors beyond his expectation. In every place and in every situation, he was favored and promoted. What Joseph did worked, and others were blessed because of him.

In the same way, we can be blessed in all that we attempt. Jesus said He would be with us, *"even unto the end of the world"*:

> *Go ye therefore, and teach all nations, baptizing them in the name of the Father, and of the Son, and of the Holy Ghost: teaching them to observe all things what-soever I have commanded you: and, lo, I am with you always, even unto the end of the world. Amen.*   Matthew 28:19-20

That is the favor God has promised you. It is His next-level endorsement:

> *For thou, LORD, wilt bless the righteous; with favour wilt thou compass him as with a shield.*   Psalm 5:12

Let that favor be evident in your life today.

TAKE THE NEXT STEP— CONSECRATION

Until you consecrate yourself to the Lord,

you limit your greatness and your impact
on the world around you:

If thou return to the Almighty, thou
shalt be built up, thou shalt put away
iniquity far from thy tabernacles. Then
shalt thou lay up gold as dust, and the
gold of Ophir as the stones of the brooks.
Yea, the Almighty shall be thy defence,
and thou shalt have plenty of silver.
Job 22:23-25

Until you separate yourself from the
world, you won't gain enough speed to get
ahead:

In the house of the righteous is much
treasure: but in the revenues of the
wicked is trouble. Proverbs 15:6

Redemption requires separation from sin
and filthiness:

Ye adulterers and adulteresses, know ye
not that the friendship of the world is

*enmity with God? whosoever therefore
will be a friend of the world is the enemy
of God.* James 4:4

*Turn you at my reproof: behold, I will
pour out my spirit unto you, I will make
known my words unto you. Because
I have called, and ye refused; I have
stretched out my hand, and no man re-
garded; but ye have set at nought all my
counsel, and would none of my reproof:
I also will laugh at your calamity; I will
mock when your fear cometh.*
Proverbs 1:23-26

Sin dulls your life and makes you a
reproach:

*Righteousness exalteth a nation: but sin
is a reproach to any people.*
Proverbs 14:34

If there is sin in your life, all you have to
do is repent of it and ask God for His mercy.
He will hear your cry and restore you.

A top spot has been reserved for you, but Satan is determined to steal your place. If you lack genuine consecration, he may well succeed. When Joseph was sorely tempted, he resisted, saying, *"How then can I do this great wickedness, and sin against God?"* (Genesis 39:9, NKJV). What are the things you know in your own life that are sins against God? Repent of them now, and God's grace is sufficient to erase your guilt and exalt you beyond measure.

Only a fool mocks at sin, thinking "It's just one of those things":

> *Fools make a mock at sin: but among the righteous there is favour.*
>
> Proverbs 14:9

The common saying is "Everyone does it," but God's truth is: Everyone will one day stand before Him and give an account of every word and deed.

You are destined for more. Take stock of your life, and then move forward in God. He loves you passionately and wants to see you at the top.

For our sakes He has said:

Be ye not unequally yoked together with unbelievers: for what fellowship hath righteousness with unrighteousness? and what communion hath light with darkness? And what concord hath Christ with Belial? or what part hath he that believeth with an infidel? And what agreement hath the temple of God with idols? for ye are the temple of the living God; as God hath said, I will dwell in them, and walk in them; and I will be their God, and they shall be my people. Wherefore come out from among them, and be ye separate, saith the Lord, and touch not the unclean thing; and I will receive you. And will be a Father unto you, and ye shall be my sons and daughters, saith the Lord Almighty.

2 Corinthians 6:14-18

There is a seed of greatness in you, and you cannot, therefore, afford to die not having attained your destined post in life.

The situations around you will try to pull you down. Satan and people will try to put you into their mould. But that's not for you. Remember, God created the Universe, and now He has entrusted you with His power to create your world. That power is inside you right now:

> *Blessed is the man that trusteth in the LORD, and whose hope the LORD is. For he shall be as a tree planted by the waters, and that spreadeth out her roots by the river, and shall not see when heat cometh, but her leaf shall be green; and shall not be careful in the year of drought, neither shall cease from yielding fruit.* Jeremiah 17:7-8

You are too loaded to become a misfit, and God doesn't create any nonentities. You are here to be a blessing and a joy to your generation and to many generations to come:

> *Whereas thou has been forsaken and hated, so that no man went through*

> *thee, I will make thee an eternal excellency, a joy of many generations.*
>
> Isaiah 60:15

You are *"fearfully and wonderfully made"* (Psalm 139:14), and God created you with precise intent. Therefore, you are not just some left-over. Out of everything He had created, when it came to man, He used the words *"very good"*:

> *And God saw every thing that he had made, and, behold, it was very good. And the evening and the morning were the sixth day.* Genesis 1:31

So, what should you do? Tap into the resources available for your consumption and use them to grow and excel in life. God is committed to "more than enough," so don't limit Him by your level of thinking.

Negative ideas come about as a results of the lies the enemy tells in an attempt to reduce you to his standard, but a perfect God could not create an imperfect being. You are complete for what you were created to become:

> *And ye are complete in him, which is the head of all principality and power.*
> Colossians 2:10

Avoid competition with others. You are a winner in your own lane. Improve on yourself, and others will line up to watch you perform.

You are *Destined for Greatness*, but there are things you must understand and put into practice in order to become outstanding.

CHAPTER 11

DIVINE WISDOM IS KEY TO YOUR SUCCESS

*And wisdom and knowledge shall be the stability of thy times, and strength of salvation: the fear of the L*ORD* is his treasure.* Isaiah 33:6

Going to the next level is impossible without divine wisdom. It is key to your stability, prosperity, and happiness.

A wise person is mightier than a physically strong person:

A wise man is strong; yea, a man of knowledge increaseth strength.
Proverbs 24:5

The exceptional life of Jesus on Earth was characterized by divine wisdom. He lived a life no man had ever lived, and none could match the level of His results. He was filled with wisdom and favor from a very early age:

> *And the child grew, and waxed strong in spirit, filled with wisdom: and the grace of God was upon him.* Luke 2:40

Wisdom is taping into God's way of doing things. Men said about Jesus, *"What wisdom is this ... that even such mighty works are wrought by his hands"*:

> *And when the sabbath day was come, he began to teach in the synagogue: and many hearing him were astonished, saying, From whence hath this man these things? and what wisdom is this which is given unto him, that even such mighty works are wrought by his hands?* Mark 6:2

This same wisdom is available to us for next-level results today:

> *But of him are ye in Christ Jesus, who of God is made unto us wisdom, and righteousness, and sanctification, and redemption.* 1 Corinthians 1:30

If you haven't yet seen the manifestation of divine wisdom in your life, you can have it now for the asking:

> *If any of you lack wisdom, let him ask of God, that giveth to all men liberally, and upbraideth not; and it shall be given him.* James 1:5

God's wisdom is not scientific; it is supernatural. Although it is simple, it produces amazing results.

When an axe head fell into the water in the time of Elisha, the man of God told his companions to cut a stick and throw it into the river. The result was that the axe head floated to the top and was retrieved. That wasn't scientific at all; it was divine and supernatural (see 2 Kings 6).

It takes faith in the simplicity of the wisdom of God to see results, for very often what God shows us seems too simple, too easy to be real. It involves hearing the Word of God and then doing what God has said:

> *Therefore whosoever heareth these sayings of mine, and doeth them, I will liken him unto a wise man, which built his house upon a rock.* Matthew 7:24

When Jesus got into Peter's boat and told him to cast his nets, Peter said to Jesus:

> *Master, we have toiled all the night, and have taken nothing: nevertheless at thy word I will let down the net.* Luke 5:5

That was divine wisdom at work. James wrote to the early churches:

> *Is any sick among you? let him call for the elders of the church; and let them*

pray over him, anointing him with oil in the name of the Lord: and the prayer of faith shall save the sick, and the Lord shall raise him up; and if he have committed sins, they shall be forgiven him.
James 5:14-15

Even from earliest Old Testament times the wisdom of God was evident in those who loved and served Him. For example, Isaac:

Then Isaac sowed in that land, and received in the same year an hundredfold: and the LORD blessed him. And the man waxed great, and went forward, and grew until he became very great: for he had possession of flocks, and possession of herds, and great store of servants: and the Philistines envied him.
Genesis 26:12-14

If you want to live long, honor your father and your mother:

Children, obey your parents in the Lord: for this is right. Honour thy father and

*mother; which is the first commandment
with promise.*   Ephesians 6:1-2

If you want extraordinary results, sit down
first and do some thinking and planning:

*For which of you, intending to build a
tower, sitteth not down first, and coun-
teth the cost, whether he have sufficient
to finish it?*   Luke 14:28

God's great wisdom is revealed to our
glory:

*But we speak the wisdom of God in a
mystery, even the hidden wisdom, which
God ordained before the world unto our
glory: which none of the princes of this
world knew: for had they known it, they
would not have crucified the Lord of
glory. But as it is written, Eye hath not
seen, nor ear heard, neither have entered
into the heart of man, the things which
God hath prepared for them that love
him.*   1 Corinthians 2:7-9

APPLY THE MYSTERY OF PRAYER

Wisdom can be acquired through the mystery of prayer. Every upward change of status requires prayer as a lifestyle. You will never be bound or successfully resisted unless your prayer life had died or is in a coma:

Verily, verily, I say unto you, He that believeth on me, the works that I do shall he do also; and greater works than these shall he do; because I go unto my Father. And whatsoever ye shall ask in my name, that will I do, that the Father may be glorified in the Son. If ye shall ask any thing in my name, I will do it.
John 14:12-14

You can change your level of achievement by engaging Heaven to send down its resources:

Call unto me, and I will answer thee, and show thee great and mighty things, which thou knowest not. Jeremiah 33:3

223

Confess your sins to each other and pray for each other so that you may be healed. The earnest prayer of a righteous person has great power and produces wonderful results. Elijah was as human as we are, and yet when he prayed earnestly that no rain would fall, none fell for three and a half years! Then, when he prayed again, the sky sent down rain and the earth began to yield its crops.

James 5:16-18, NLT

It's time to pray and change the story of your life. Laziness in prayer equals stagnation in life. Jesus prayed, and even His countenance changed:

And it came to pass about an eight days after these sayings, he took Peter and John and James, and went up into a mountain to pray. And as he prayed, the fashion of his countenance was altered, and his raiment was white and glistering.   Luke 9:28-29

Jabez was cursed, but he changed his story through prayer (see 1 Chronicles 4). Are you doing something about your case? Prayer makes your life too hot for Satan to handle.

BE MINDFUL OF WHAT YOU ARE CARRYING

As you open yourself to God's wisdom, be mindful of the value of what you are carrying and protect it. None of us is born empty. We are all born with substance to produce a desired destiny. But life is governed by the principles of God:

> *And God said, Let the earth bring forth grass, the herb yielding seed, and the fruit tree yielding fruit after his kind, whose seed is in itself, upon the earth: and it was so.* Genesis 1:11

Inside every cow there is a herd, inside every tree there is a forest, and inside every man there is God. For every product, there is a parent material. Seeds produce after their kind.

God designed you for greatness because there is no smallness in God. Look inward, for there is something in you just crying to be released. The reason you are worried at times and uncomfortable is because your time has come. The pregnancy of your greatness has already matured, and the baby is about to come out. That's why you feel so restless. Get ready to expand on every side.

If you can't sleep, rise and shine for your light is come and the glory of God is risen upon you. God knew and believed in what He put inside of you. That was His investment to rule the Earth through you. Now He allows situations to come your way to provoke you to action.

God brought all the animals to Adam, to see what he would call them:

> *And out of the ground the LORD God formed every beast of the field, and every fowl of the air; and brought them unto Adam to see what he would call them: and whatsoever Adam called*

every living creature, that was the name thereof.   Genesis 2:19

Did Adam know he had this ability? Probably not. It might surprise you what you carry that you have not yet used. Release it now in the name of Jesus Christ.

BE WHO GOD MADE YOU TO BE

Take the pressure off of your life by being who and what God designed you to be. Trying to be someone else or do what someone else does creates unnecessary pressures. Being who you were destined to be, however, takes your cooperation with God.

A goat can never be a cat, even if it is raised in the same house and eats the same food. The nature and the characteristics of a goat are different than those of a cat. Your uniqueness is real, and that's what glorifies God. The next level starts with a mindset that is glued to the Word of God, based upon your intended identity, and filled with heavenly wisdom:

For as he thinketh in his heart, so is he: Eat and drink, saith he to thee; but his heart is not with thee.

Proverbs 23:7

You are fully equipped for your destiny. A cat is designed and equipped to meow, a lion is designed and equipped to roar, and you are designed and equipped to rule:

Thou madest him to have dominion over the works of thy hands; thou hast put all things under his feet.

Psalm 8:6

AVOID THE PITFALLS

Distraction is the greatest weapon in the hand of the devil to stop a person's greatness, and competition is what it uses. If you don't know who you are and who you're not, you may spend your life competing with others. There is nothing ordinary about you. Avoid these pitfalls.

SHARPEN YOUR GIFTS

Sharpen your gifts, for they will take you to the top. It was not David's singing skills that took him to the throne. It was his shepherding skills, specifically his mastery of the slingshot. That doesn't sound very important, but what you have neglected about yourself just might be the instrument of ultimate greatness. Don't give up on who God made you to be, get His wisdom for day to day living, and strive to conquer every giant in your way.

You are *Destined for Greatness,* but there are things you must understand and put into practice in order to become outstanding.

CHAPTER 12

YOU HAVE THE POWER

Who through faith subdued king-doms, wrought righteousness, obtained promises, stopped the mouths of lions. Quenched the violence of fire, escaped the edge of the sword, out of weakness were made strong, waxed valiant in fight, turned to flight the armies of the aliens. Women received their dead raised to life again: and others were tortured, not accepting deliverance; that they might obtain a better resurrection.

Hebrews 11:33-35

You have that same power. Where does your power come from?

THE POWER OF FAITH

Faith is designed to clear obstacles and subdue every opposition to our destiny. It was by faith that men of old subdue kingdoms. Why did they do that? Because God said it, and therefore it had to be done. They were acting on the Word of God, and that produces results every time. You have this faith resident in you now. Put it to work:

> *For I say, through the grace given unto me, to every man that is among you, not to think of himself more highly than he ought to think; but to think soberly, according as God hath dealt to every man the measure of faith.*   Romans 12:3

Your commission comes with the grace and unction needed to root out whatever stands in your way. Let every enemy be moved in Jesus' name:

> *Then the LORD put forth his hand, and touched my mouth. And the LORD said*

unto me, Behold, I have put my words in thy mouth. See, I have this day set thee over the nations and over the kingdoms, to root out, and to pull down, and to destroy, and to throw down, to build, and to plant.   Jeremiah 1:9-10

You cannot allow anything to stop you from ruling the Earth. You are not doing it for a selfish cause, but for God. You are the one He has sent and recognized as His servant. Your faith, therefore, is a partnership with God, and the goal is to bring His counsel to pass on this fallen planet:

Thou art my battle axe and weapons of war: for with thee will I break in pieces the nations, and with thee will I destroy kingdoms; and with thee will I break in pieces the horse and his rider; and with thee will I break in pieces the chariot and his rider; with thee also will I break in pieces man and woman; and with thee will I break in pieces old and young; and with thee will I break in pieces the

> *young man and the maid; I will also*
> *break in pieces with thee the shepherd*
> *and his flock; and with thee will I break*
> *in pieces the husbandman and his yoke of*
> *oxen; and with thee will I break in pieces*
> *captains and rulers.*
> *And I will render unto Babylon and to all*
> *the inhabitants of Chaldea all their evil*
> *that they have done in Zion in your sight,*
> *saith the* LORD. Jeremiah 51:20-24

Agreeing with God will put everything you need at your feet. He is the Doer, and you are His representative. Tap into the power that is available now, and quickly move to the next level.

The woman with the issue of blood saw something in Jesus that she needed, and this caused her to press until she reached Him and received His touch:

> *And, behold, a woman, which was*
> *diseased with an issue of blood twelve*
> *years, came behind him, and touched the*
> *hem of his garment: for she said within*

herself, If I may but touch his garment,
I shall be whole.   Matthew 9:20-21

You must see something in Jesus you need too and then release your faith to receive it. There is a tendency to be discouraged because what we are experiencing doesn't look like what God said. Please don't be discouraged. Greatness is in you. You just need to get the touch of the Master on your life. Then everything will change.

God told Abraham that nations were in him, and yet his wife, Sarah, was barren. She was also getting older. Still God said, *"kings shall come out of thee"*:

> *As for me, behold, my covenant is with thee,*
> *and thou shalt be a father of many nations.*
> *Neither shall thy name any more be called*
> *Abram, but thy name shall be Abraham; for*
> *a father of many nations have I made thee.*
> *And I will make thee exceeding fruitful, and*
> *I will make nations of thee, and kings shall*
> *come out of thee. And I will establish my*
> *covenant between me and thee and thy seed*

> *after thee in their generations for an everlast-*
> *ing covenant, to be a God unto thee, and to*
> *thy seed after thee.*   Genesis 17:4-7

The kings in you cannot be allowed to die without ever being born. Release your faith into God's Word. By means of your prayer requests or desires, create a picture in your mind of the desired outcome, trust God, and then see how He works wonders on your behalf.

THE POWER OF KNOWLEDGE

In order to be in command, you need knowledge and lots of it. What you don't know is the reason for your frustrations. Knowledge brings fulfillment.

Unfortunately, knowledge cannot be imparted by the laying on of hands; it can only be acquired through study. This is where many fail. They are lazy and don't want to take responsibility, so they are doomed to live their lives in mediocrity.

Worse, many fall into captivity because they have lost their command by a failure to seek truth:

> *Therefore my people are gone into captivity, because they have no knowledge: and their honourable men are famished, and their multitude dried up with thirst.* Isaiah 5:13

To many, prayer and study seems like a waste of time, and that explains why so many of God's people lack the knowledge of the truth. In any area of your life where you feel incompetent or inadequate, look for material to study on that subject. It's available. You just need to find it.

It is not enough to know something. You must know it until you know that you know it.

Jesus wept over Jerusalem because of the ignorance that had kept her people in bondage:

> *And when he was come near, he beheld the city, and wept over it, saying, If thou hadst known, even thou, at least in this*

> *thy day, the things which belong unto*
> *thy peace! but now they are hid from*
> *thine eyes.* Luke 19:41-42

How sad! Don't let that be your end. Peace was there, but these people were still troubled. Today, the God of your fathers is there with you. Be at peace!

Those of us who are in Christ Jesus are never limited in life by the devil; we are only limited by our own ignorance. Never fear Satan, and never fear sickness or death, but do fear ignorance. It is the pathway to bondage:

> *My people are destroyed for lack of*
> *knowledge: because thou hast rejected*
> *knowledge, I will also reject thee, that*
> *thou shalt be no priest to me: seeing thou*
> *hast forgotten the law of thy God, I will*
> *also forget thy children.* Hosea 4:6

When Jesus came to His own, they rejected Him:

> *He was in the world, and the world was*
> *made by him, and the world knew him*

not. He came unto his own, and his own received him not. But as many as received him, to them gave he power to become the sons of God, even to them that believe on his name. John 1:10-12

Knowledge gives you practical control over everything around you. In the midst of storms, Paul spoke:

But after long abstinence Paul stood forth in the midst of them, and said, Sirs, ye should have hearkened unto me, and not have loosed from Crete, and to have gained this harm and loss. And now I exhort you to be of good cheer: for there shall be no loss of any man's life among you, but of the ship. For there stood by me this night the angel of God, whose I am, and whom I serve, saying, Fear not, Paul; thou must be brought before Caesar: and, lo, God hath given thee all them that sail with thee. Wherefore, sirs, be of good cheer: for I believe God, that it shall be even as it was told me. Acts 27:21-25

You and I have that same standing in Heaven. Redemption has brought us back into the Garden of God, and there is no harassment here. So, go for it by going for more knowledge.

THE POWER OF THE HOLY SPIRIT

Power from on high is the key to scaling up to higher levels. Mary was told by the angel that the power from on high would overshadow her, and the holy thing that would be born of her would be called *"the Son of God"*:

> *And the angel answered and said unto her, The Holy Ghost shall come upon thee, and the power of the Highest shall overshadow thee: therefore also that holy thing which shall be born of thee shall be called the Son of God.* Luke 1:35

The Holy Spirit will also birth things, wonderful things, through you. These will be things you could never do by your own power or strength. In Mary's day, there was great darkness, but suddenly, because she yielded to the Spirit's control, light came. You cannot be filled with the Spirit of God and remain confused:

> *In the beginning God created the heaven and the earth. And the earth was without form, and void; and darkness was upon the face of the deep. And the Spirit of God moved upon the face of the waters. And God said, Let there be light: and there was light.* Genesis 1:1-3

God's Word says:

> *Now the Lord is that Spirit: and where the Spirit of the Lord is, there is liberty.* 2 Corinthians 3:17

God's Spirit is with you and in you. Therefore, bondage must end now in the name of Jesus Christ. Resident on the inside of you is the very creative force of God:

Thou sendest forth thy spirit, they are created: and thou renewest the face of the earth.   Psalm 104:30

And I will pray the Father, and he shall give you another Comforter, that he may abide with you for ever; even the Spirit of truth; whom the world cannot receive, because it seeth him not, neither knoweth him: but ye know him; for he dwelleth with you, and shall be in you. I will not leave you comfortless: I will come to you.   John 14:16-18

One of the major deceptions of the enemy is to convince us to look at every issues from a natural standpoint. There is a spiritual dimension to everything in life, even if you caused it to happen by your own actions:

And ought not this woman, being a daughter of Abraham, whom Satan hath bound, lo, these eighteen years, be loosed from this bond on the sabbath day?
Luke 13:16

And one of the multitude answered and said, Master, I have brought unto thee my son, which hath a dumb spirit; and wheresoever he taketh him, he teareth him: and he foameth, and gnasheth with his teeth, and pineth away: and I spake to thy disciples that they should cast him out; and they could not.

He answereth him, and saith, O faithless generation, how long shall I be with you? how long shall I suffer you? bring him unto me.

And they brought him unto him: and when he saw him, straightway the spirit tare him; and he fell on the ground, and wallowed foaming.

And he asked his father, How long is it ago since this came unto him?

And he said, Of a child. And ofttimes it hath cast him into the fire, and into the waters, to destroy him: but if thou canst do any thing, have compassion on us, and help us.

Jesus said unto him, If thou canst believe, all things are possible to him that believeth.

And straightway the father of the child cried out, and said with tears, Lord, I believe; help thou mine unbelief.

When Jesus saw that the people came running together, he rebuked the foul spirit, saying unto him, Thou dumb and deaf spirit, I charge thee, come out of him, and enter no more into him.

And the spirit cried, and rent him sore, and came out of him: and he was as one dead; insomuch that many said, He is dead.

But Jesus took him by the hand, and lifted him up; and he arose.   Mark 9:17-27

As believers in Christ, when we face obstacles, we must not panic. Our Father has us covered — always. We will get through this trial, and He will receive all the glory:

My Father, which gave them me, is greater than all; and no man is able to pluck them out of my Father's hand.
John 10:29

This sonship mindset is your key to a new song in life. Moses' attitude when facing the feared Pharaoh was, "How dare you try to stop us! Our Father is Almighty God! Let us go, or He will kill you":

> *And thou shalt say unto Pharaoh, Thus saith the* LORD, *Israel is my son, even my firstborn: and I say unto thee, Let my son go, that he may serve me: and if thou refuse to let him go, behold, I will slay thy son, even thy firstborn.*
>
> Exodus 4:22-23

God's love for His people is beyond human comprehension. He would never allow you to be famished. It might appear that there is no way out of a given situation, but there is always a way with God. Stop saying, "Why me?" God has prepared an escape route for you to be completely free of the threat:

> *There hath no temptation taken you but such as is common to man: but God is*

> *faithful, who will not suffer you to be tempted above that ye are able; but will with the temptation also make a way to escape, that ye may be able to bear it.*
>
> 1 Corinthians 10:13

Life's situations are not what they appear to be, so refuse to be intimidated. You are more than victorious through Jesus Christ:

> *Then all the Midianites and the Amalekites and the children of the east were gathered together, and went over, and pitched in the valley of Jezreel.*
>
> Judges 6:33

> *Now Zebah and Zalmunna were in Karkor, and their hosts with them, about fifteen thousand men, all that were left of all the hosts of the children of the east: for there fell an hundred and twenty thousand men that drew sword.*
>
> Judges 8:10

These Midianites had 135,000 soldiers, and that must have been intimidating, but Gideon called for volunteers to come and fight them. God, however, told him not to accept every warrior:

> *Now therefore go to, proclaim in the ears of the people, saying, Whosoever is fearful and afraid, let him return and depart early from mount Gilead. And there returned of the people twenty and two thousand; and there remained ten thousand.* Judges 7:3

Only 32,000 men had shown up, but God said there were too many. How could that be? In the end, God needed only 300 men, and what He would do through them was a marvel. That same God is with you every day, and nothing will stop your glory from shining forth in the name of Jesus Christ.

You are *Destined for Greatness*, but there are things you must understand and put into practice in order to become outstanding.

CHAPTER 13

SEEKING DIVINE GUIDANCE

There is a way which seemeth right unto a man, but the end thereof are the ways of death. Proverbs 14:12

Without divine direction, life is filled with much turmoil, confusion, and chaos. Why? Because what seems good to man ends in death. It ends with men and women as wanderers:

As a bird that wandereth from her nest, so is a man that wandereth from his place. Proverbs 27:8

Those who dwell in God's Word, however, never lose the way:

> *Thy word is a lamp unto my feet, and a light unto my path.*   Psalm 119:105

Never forget: the next level order of results is a function of favor, but divine direction is what it relies upon. This is possible when God becomes the center of everything in our lives. He told His prophet, *"Arise, and get thee to Zarephath"*:

> *Arise, get thee to Zarephath, which belongeth to Zidon, and dwell there: behold, I have commanded a widow woman there to sustain thee. So he arose and went to Zarephath. And when he came to the gate of the city, behold, the widow woman was there gathering of sticks: and he called to her, and said, Fetch me, I pray thee, a little water in a vessel, that I may drink.*
> 1 Kings 17:9-10

This didn't seem to make good sense, but prophets became great because they were willing to say and do unusual things:

And Elijah the Tishbite, who was of the inhabitants of Gilead, said unto Ahab, As the LORD God of Israel liveth, before whom I stand, there shall not be dew nor rain these years, but according to my word.   1 Kings 17:1

And he said, I have been very jealous for the LORD God of hosts: for the children of Israel have forsaken thy covenant, thrown down thine altars, and slain thy prophets with the sword; and I, even I only, am left; and they seek my life, to take it away.   1 Kings 19:10

Jesus said, *"Seek ye first the kingdom of God"*:

But seek ye first the kingdom of God, and his righteousness; and all these things shall be added unto you.
                Matthew 6:33

Your commitment to God and to the course of His Kingdom offers you a great platform for divine leadership:

And lead us not into temptation, but deliver us from evil: for thine is the kingdom, and the power, and the glory, for ever. Amen. Matthew 6:13

Jesus said we should pray, *"Lead us not into temptation."* Divine leading is the heritage of the redeemed:

And thine ears shall hear a word behind thee, saying, This is the way, walk ye in it, when ye turn to the right hand, and when ye turn to the left. Isaiah 30:21

GOD MAY GUIDE YOU THROUGH VISION AND DREAMS

If you don't know where you're going, you will miss God's favor, help, and support. Without a dream, every destiny is doomed. The Bible says very clearly:

Where there is no vision, the people perish: but he that keepeth the law, happy is he. Proverbs 29:18

It does not say, "Where there is no money." It is vision that gives direction to life, not money. Vision enables you to maximize your time and energy. Don't allow any obstacle or any limitation to stop you from dreaming. Nothing can stop you when God is with you and for you.

Seeing the devastating situation of a blind man, Jesus asked him, "What do you want me to do for you?"

> *And Jesus answered and said unto him, What wilt thou that I should do unto thee? The blind man said unto him, Lord, that I might receive my sight.*
>
> Mark 10:51

And Jesus is asking us the same question. It's all about vision. Don't just pray. Know what you want. Know your desires. Then believe God for a total turnaround in your situation.

Martha of Bethany said to Jesus:

> *Then said Martha unto Jesus, Lord, if thou hadst been here, my brother had*

> *not died. But I know, that even now,*
> *whatsoever thou wilt ask of God, God*
> *will give it thee. Jesus saith unto her,*
> *Thy brother shall rise again.*
>
> John 11:21-23

Don't worry about what might have been. Jesus is with you now, so let Him work it all out. God will give you the inspiration, but you have to do the dreaming. What do you want God to do for you? Dreams can not only keep you alive; they can birth goal setting and planning and raise up others to help you achieve your destiny.

GOD WILL GUIDE YOU INTO SERVICE

Kingdom service is your key to experiencing the next level without any hinderance. The truth that you must understand is this: God knows what you need before you ever ask Him. Jesus said this:

> *But when ye pray, use not vain repeti-*
> *tions, as the heathen do: for they think*

that they shall be heard for their much speaking. Be not ye therefore like unto them: for your Father knoweth what things ye have need of, before ye ask him.
Matthew 6:7-8

He knows, so ask in faith, and then lay hold of the answers He provides. The world is exhausting itself running after "stuff," but you are receiving everything you need through faith and your relationship to a loving heavenly Father.

Even the devil can't stop God's servants. God places a line of demarcation between you and all evil:

Then shall ye return, and discern between the righteous and the wicked, between him that serveth God and him that serveth him not. Malachi 3:18

There is no shortcut to living a life of peace and joy in serving God without ulterior motives and with sincerity of heart. You do this, not just because of what you want to get from God, but because you are wholly committed to Him and His love:

Sixteen years old was Uzziah when he began to reign, and he reigned fifty and two years in Jerusalem. His mother's name also was Jecoliah of Jerusalem. And he did that which was right in the sight of the LORD, according to all that his father Amaziah did. And he sought God in the days of Zechariah, who had understanding in the visions of God: and as long as he sought the LORD, God made him to prosper.

And God helped him against the Philistines, and against the Arabians that dwelt in Gurbaal, and the Mehunims.

Also he built towers in the desert, and digged many wells: for he had much cattle, both in the low country, and in the plains: husbandmen also, and vine dressers in the mountains, and in Carmel: for he loved husbandry.

And he made in Jerusalem engines,

invented by cunning men, to be on the towers and upon the bulwarks, to shoot arrows and great stones withal. And his name spread far abroad; for he was marvellously helped, till he was strong.
                  2 Chronicles 26:3-5, 7, 10 and 15

And ye shall serve the LORD your God, and he shall bless thy bread, and thy water; and I will take sickness away from the midst of thee. There shall nothing cast their young, nor be barren, in thy land: the number of thy days I will fulfil.   Exodus 23:25-26

All of these blessings come to those who refuse to serve two masters, but make God the center of their lives. They will never be ignored.

Serving God changed the life of Peter. Simon without destiny became a pillar of the Church, and it's now your turn. What can you do? Start by winning souls, evangelizing others, giving, and in this way, using your gifts and talents to further God's Kingdom. Let your impact be felt.

The reason God told Pharaoh He would kill him was that He wanted His people to serve Him, and nothing could stand in their way. As they served Him, God would destroy their adversaries. And the same is true today.

When we understand God's plan for man, we realize that He gave man much more than intelligence. He gave him everything he needed to manage the Earth. God didn't just want man to be smart; He wanted us to be creative, so He gave us the mental and spiritual capacity to subdue (control) life. That was the nature of our Father in us.

Adam could name all the animals in the world without ever consulting a book:

> *And the* Lord *God formed man of the dust of the ground, and breathed into his nostrils the breath of life; and man became a living soul.*
>
> Genesis 2:7

"But," God told him, "the day you eat the fruit of the tree of the knowledge of good and evil, you will surely die." He would lose the connection that made him superior to every other creature. That "death" was the reason for all future failure. Man had not been programmed to fail. In fact, the life of God in him forbid it:

> *That whosoever believeth in him should not perish, but have eternal life.*
> John 3:15

> *And I give unto them eternal life; and they shall never perish, neither shall any man pluck them out of my hand.*
> John 10:28

Satan was never Adam's issue; it was his own disobedience. That was why God had warned him, and we can see that he understood God's instructions:

> *And Adam was not deceived, but the woman being deceived was in the transgression.*
> 1 Timothy 2:14

The death of Jesus on the cross of Calvary was God Himself becoming one with death, to free mankind and reconnect him to the foundation of the life he was created for. What man needed was not money or a great business. He needed life. He was dead spiritually, and his connection to the Source of all life was lost. Jesus came to introduce life back to us, so that we could once again live with creativity and results:

> *The thief cometh not, but for to steal, and to kill, and to destroy: I am come that they might have life, and that they might have it more abundantly.*
>
> John 10:10

> *He that believeth on the Son of God hath the witness in himself: he that believeth not God hath made him a liar; because he believeth not the record that God gave of his Son. And this is the record, that God hath given to us eternal life, and this life is in his Son. He that hath the Son hath life; and he*

*that hath not the Son of God hath not
life.*   1 John 5:10-12

That is the mindset that destroys failure
and every limitation in life. Now that the life
of God resides in you, you can do anything
He tells you to do, and you can do it well
for His glory.

You are *Destined for Greatness,* but there are
things you must understand and put into
practice in order to become outstanding.

CHAPTER 14

DARE TO BE A DREAMER

And the LORD answered me, and said, Write the vision, and make it plain upon tables, that he may run that readeth it. For the vision is yet for an appointed time, but at the end it shall speak, and not lie: though it tarry, wait for it; because it will surely come, it will not tarry. Habakkuk 2:2-3

Without a dream, there is no future, no push, and no enthusiasm. The major catalyst for depression is dreamlessness, which gives birth to hopelessness. Without a destination in mind, it's difficult to travel.

I know that you pray, you fast, and you give, but where is your dream? People are not stagnated because God hates them or even because Satan has attacked them. It's because they have no dream. Without a dream, man's destiny is doomed:

> *And the* Lord *said unto Abram, after that Lot was separated from him, Lift up now thine eyes, and look from the place where thou art northward, and southward, and eastward, and westward: for all the land which thou seest, to thee will I give it, and to thy seed for ever. And I will make thy seed as the dust of the earth: so that if a man can number the dust of the earth, then shall thy seed also be numbered.*   Genesis 13:14-16

Knowing where you are going wakes up the giants in you. It connects the dots and makes you alive to your destiny. The reason for a prayerless and faithless lifestyle is the lack of a dream. If you are a dreamer and the dream is real to you, you will pray, and you will plan.

Every greatness is tied to a dream. Even Jesus had a dream in mind:

Looking unto Jesus the author and finisher of our faith; who for the joy that was set before him endured the cross, despising the shame, and is set down at the right hand of the throne of God. Hebrews 12:2

He did it *"for the joy that was set before him."* When it seems that every hope is lost, doors have closed to you, and you begin to live at the mercy of your situation, all that can save you is a dream. A dream is something that come to you often, almost becoming an obsession. Don't dismiss it. Write it down. It means that God is stirring something in you.

CREATE A PROPER ENVIRONMENT

The foundation for innovation is a mind that is connected to God. Our minds were designed to be the continuation of creativity and invention:

For who hath known the mind of the Lord, that he may instruct him? but we have the mind of Christ. 1 Corinthians 2:16

265

What limits the creativity and greatness that is in you as a child of God is your level of exposure and is dependent upon your environment. If you change your environment or manage it, you can unleash your potential. If you change your environment, then what is already in you will grow.

The psalmist created such an atmosphere:

> *I will sing of mercy and judgment: unto thee, O Lord, will I sing. I will behave myself wisely in a perfect way. O when wilt thou come unto me?*
>
> *I will walk within my house with a perfect heart. I will set no wicked thing before mine eyes:*
>
> *I hate the work of them that turn aside; it shall not cleave to me. A froward heart shall depart from me: I will not know a wicked person.*
>
> *Whoso privily slandereth his neighbour, him will I cut off: him that hath an high look and a proud heart will not I suffer. Mine eyes shall be upon the faithful of the land, that they may dwell with me:*

he that walketh in a perfect way, he shall serve me.

He that worketh deceit shall not dwell within my house: he that telleth lies shall not tarry in my sight.

I will early destroy all the wicked of the land; that I may cut off all wicked doers from the city of the LORD.   Psalm 101:1-8

That's what it means to consciously create an environment for God to cause your potential to manifest. Run from joyless environments; they will choke the life out of you. Run from toxic and negative environments; they will kill your dream. Seek out people who inspire you, books that wake you up, relationships that challenge you to greatness, people who create in you a hunger for more of the things of God. Until your environment changes, you will continue to eat thorns.

DEVELOP CRITICAL THINKING SKILLS

Thinkers are rulers, and your thinking will determine your living, for it provokes what is inside of you. Godly thinking causes us to be careful to check and double-check our information—what we see, experience, contemplate, and talk about—so that we can make good decisions about what we believe and do.

An influential definition comes from the Foundation for Critical Thinking, which views good thinking as "a careful way of thinking where you purposely judge things. This thinking looks at facts, situations, ideas, ways, and standards."[1] What's the essence we gather from this definition? At its core, critical thinking is a deliberate process of examining, understanding, and evaluating information in a methodical manner. There can be no constructive approach to life without critical thinking. Our thinking must not be negative, and it must use the facts provided to get results. God said:

> *For as he thinketh in his heart, so is he:*
> *Eat and drink, saith he to thee; but his*
> *heart is not with thee.*   Proverbs 23:7

---

1. https://www.criticalthinking.org/

For to be carnally minded is death; but to be spiritually minded is life and peace.   Romans 8:6

Spiritual thinking is discerning the truth by the help of the Holy Spirit. Understanding is the key to become outstanding, and creative thinking is the key to understanding. This shows clearly what the concepts are and how to get them applied.

What you don't understand you can't apply. Life poses questions, and inside those questions and challenges lie the answers. Without critical thinking, you will miss the point:

I call heaven and earth to record this day against you, that I have set before you life and death, blessing and cursing: therefore choose life, that both thou and thy seed may live.
                    Deuteronomy 30:19

This is what produces the choices we make in life. Thinking brings the problems under a microscope, so we can examine them and find solutions by the help of the Holy Ghost:

> *For which of you, intending to build a tower, sitteth not down first, and counteth the cost, whether he have sufficient to finish it? Lest haply, after he hath laid the foundation, and is not able to finish it, all that behold it begin to mock him.*   Luke 14:28-29

Critical thinking is the objective analysis of a concept in order to determine the correct judgement. The Holy Spirit will help us to think right, but He will not do the thinking for us. Behind every productive thought are the following:

BEING A PERSON OF CURIOSITY

Until Moses stepped aside to see what was happening with the bush that seemed to be on fire but was not being consumed, there was no voice from the Lord. Curiosity begins when you dare to ask questions in order to get answers:

"Why am I so poor?"
"Why is my business not working the
way I want it to?"
"What do I need to do to turn things
around?"

Thinking things through gives birth to searching, which leads to discovery.

BEING A PERSON OF VERITY

Be truthful. Allow the facts discovered to take the center stage of your thinking. Don't just jump to conclusions. The Bible suggests listening to what comes *"out of the mouth of two or three witnesses"*:

> *But if he will not hear thee, then take with thee one or two more, that in the mouth of two or three witnesses every word may be established.* Matthew 18:16

In this way, you can verify the truth through others who have already discovered it. We live in the age of information, but not all information is true. That's why we have to verify everything:

> *Finally, brethren, whatsoever things are true, whatsoever things are honest, whatsoever things are just, whatsoever things are pure, whatsoever things are lovely, whatsoever things are of good report; if there be any virtue, and if there be any praise, think on these things.*
> Philippians 4:8

Declare today in prayer:

Father in the name of Jesus Christ, let the glory and wonders in my life begin to manifest now.

I receive strength to subdue the earth with wisdom and divine ability today.

On my way to the top, I frustrate the plan of the wicked over my destiny now in Jesus' name.

Yes, you are *Destined for Greatness*, but there are things you must understand and put into practice in order to become outstanding.

OTHER BOOKS BY
DR. ABIOLA IDOWU

HEAVEN on EARTH

Bishop Dr. Abiola Idowu

WALKING AND LIVING IN YOUR INHERITANCE

BISHOP ABIOLA IDOWU

WEALTH
FAVOUR JOY
GOOD HEALTH
TRANSFORMATION

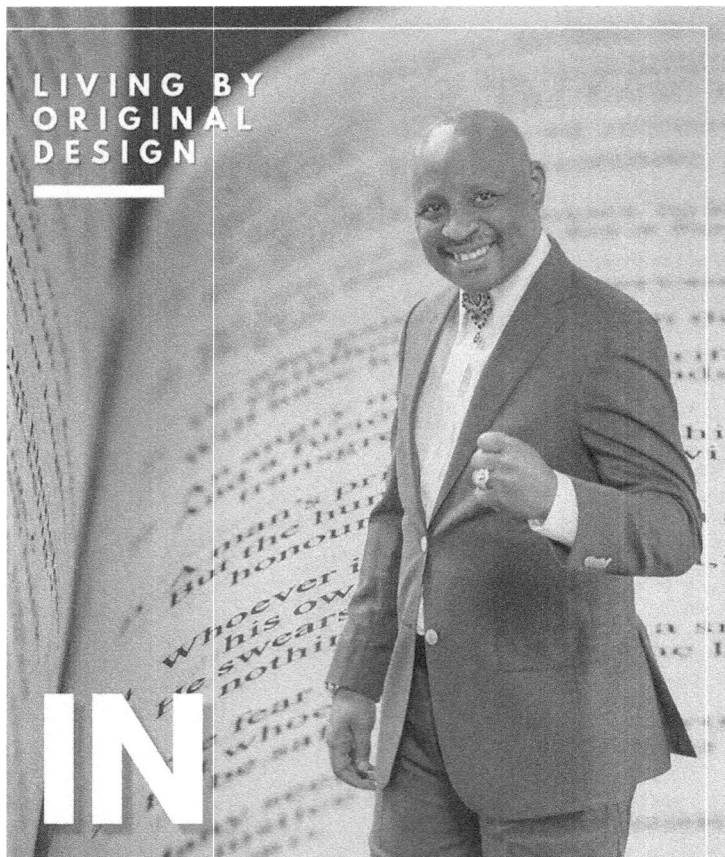

LIVING BY ORIGINAL DESIGN

IN CHARGE

BISHOP ABIOLA IDOWU

RULING Your WORLD

DR. ABIOLA IDOWU

Author Contact
Information

You may contact the author directly in the following way:

eMail: Bishopidowu@crepa.org

Telephone: (904) 469-5724

www.ingramcontent.com/pod-product-compliance
Lightning Source LLC
Chambersburg PA
CBHW030915090426
42737CB00007B/198